TERRY SCHMIDA'S

TRUE CRIME

STORIES OF KEY WEST AND THE FLORIDA KEYS

Kirstin & Tim,
Don't get caught!
Terry Schmida

Please address inquiries to Terry Schmida at keysscribe@aol.com.

Cover design: WoduMedia.com
Layout and production: Kerry Karshna

Rare first edition. Buy several copies!

10 9 8 7 6 5 4 3
ISBN 0-9674498-7-1

Photo courtesy of Monroe County Public Library

Accused double-murder suspect Roger Foster on his way to his arraignment, on April 13, 1963.

©Wright Langley

Former Key West Fire Chief Joseph 'Bum' Farto, shortly after his arrest on drug charges, on Sept. 10, 1975.

For Mom, who taught me how to write.

CONTENTS

Acknowledgements

First of all, thank you for buying this book. You're helping to support the ongoing, rich literary tradition of the Florida Keys. Be proud!

While writing this volume, I've been fortunate to receive help from many people, to whom I owe a great debt.

At the top of this list are my parents, Walter and Joanna Schmida, whose unwavering support over the years ultimately made this project possible. My mother is also an excellent proofreader; my dad, an honest and hard-working Realtor. Should you be looking to buy or sell property in the Keys, give him a call at (305) 294-3040.

Also in line for high praise are Tom and Lynda Hambright, of the Monroe County Public Library; my good friends and Key West Citizen colleagues Mandy Bolen and Rob O'Neal; and Key West author/entrepreneur David Sloan, who helped out with editing and the logistics of the book publishing process. Thanks to Kerry Karshna for a super job with the layout, and Peter Downie for his striking cover design.

Other behind-the-scenes contributions came from retired Assistant Key West Fire Marshal Alex Vega, retired Key West Police Detective Emilio "Duke" Yannacone, retired Key West Police Captain Vincent "Cat" Catala; and the late Key West Citizen columnist Dr. Herman K. Moore.

Thanks to Solares Hill Editor Nancy Klingener for the loan of her "Bum" Farto file, and to Joan Langley of the Langley Archives for photos.

And thanks to all my other friends in the Keys, who have been there for me when I needed you most, especially my girlfriend Stephanie, who provided me with a quiet place to write and edit this book.

Last, (but certainly not least,) thanks to llama farmers Roger Akers and Sandy Henning for being the kind of landlords that make it possible for starving artists to live in – and contribute to – paradise.

Introduction

My obsession with true crime began in childhood, reading Max Haines' "Crime Flashback" column in the Toronto Sun newspaper. Later on, as a college student, I found myself retracing the steps of the 1960s terrorist group the FLQ, to the sites of some of their robberies, kidnappings and bomb blasts in my Montreal neighborhood.

It became a hobby of mine to look up these old crimes at the library. I'd jot down the addresses of the crime scenes and wander past them, wondering if the current residents or business owners had any clue as to the carnage that had happened on the very spot they were now standing.

When I was promoted to the position of crime reporter at the Key West Citizen in 1997, I felt like I had arrived at my dream job. Now I was getting paid to investigate older unsolved cases, report on current misdeeds, and even laugh a little, as I compiled the daily Crime Report section. It was an exhilarating job, and it brought me into contact with other local crime buffs, which opened my eyes to some of the more notorious local crimes of days gone by. I started to dig a little deeper and before I knew it, I had uncovered a trove of largely forgotten Keys history that I'm sure Max Haines would find fascinating.

This book is the result of my efforts.

It's difficult for many new residents or visitors to believe that this peaceful and accepting place has any kind of sordid, violent history, beyond the semi-factual accounts of pirates and smugglers they've read. In reality, paradise is populated by people who are possessed, as they are everywhere, by the frailties of the human psyche, and seeking the fulfillment of primal urges.

The motivation for some crimes is easier to understand, as in the case of drug smuggling fishermen in the economically trying 1970s. It's the senseless crimes that are the most thought-provoking. What could drive a wealthy and handsome young man to kill his equally attractive new bride? Why would a depressed high school senior murder two benefactors in cold blood? And who could possibly want to leave a fiery trail of destruction through Old Town Key West, for no apparent material gain?

Trying to piece together the rationale for the evil that people do has become a national pastime in America. In a city like Key West, with such a fascinating and colorful past, exploring the history of crime and punishment provides an unusual insight into the times in which the crimes were committed. It's a potent prism through which to view the various phases of the town's development, from the rough and remote seaport it was in the 1820s, to the welcoming vacation spot it has become today.

In compiling this book, I have not lost sight of the tragic nature of many of these cases, and the fact that the perpetrators of some of the more heinous crimes have yet to face justice. For this reason, I have selected mostly older tales here, the retellings of which are unlikely to open old wounds amongst the victims or their families. Only one story, "The Hidden Evil on Big Pine Key," involves fairly recent events. It is presented in the hopes of keeping alive the search for clues into a series of horrific unsolved crimes.

So, sit back and enjoy.

And if you happen to be standing in a bookstore right now, deciding whether or not to steal this book, a word of advice: Don't do it. Or you might end up in a starring role in Vol. II!

Terry Schmida
Key West, Florida, May 2006

Photo courtesy of Monroe County Public Library

Edward and Douglas Trevor, at right, pose with two tourists at their Garrison Bight boat slip.

Murder on the High Seas

Depressed and suicidal, a Georgia lad rolled into Key West thinking life wasn't 'worth much.' Some say he never paid the price for his subsequent crimes…

Sun-drenched and idyllic, the Florida Keys have always attracted romantics, artists, dreamers and millionaires alike. Alas, they've also attracted many of the shady characters mentioned in this book. And then there are those who come here because they've decided they want to be surrounded by palm trees and caressed by gentle, warm breezes when they pull a trigger, pop an overdose of sleeping pills, or string up a noose – and end their own unhappy lives.

"From my earliest days on the force, right up until my retirement, suicides were always more prevalent than homicides," says retired Key West Police Detective Emilio "Duke" Yannacone. "And most of them came here from someplace else to do the deed. I figured they were ashamed to do it in their homes or hometowns."

Perhaps it's that sense of shame that keeps most suicides fairly straightforward and easy for the police to make sense of: Someone checks into a hotel, writes a note, and then commits his or her last desperate act.

For one brief moment in the mid-1960s, however, Key West police found themselves dealing with one of the most unorthodox and unfortunate suicide cases in the city's history, one that ended badly for all involved.

• • •

In the early afternoon of April 11, 1963, Key West charter boat captain Douglas Trevor and his son and first mate Edward, pulled out of Garrison Bight in thier 32-foot Norseman vessel Dream Girl. Aboard for the scheduled five-hour trip was a single passenger neither Trevor had ever seen before: An enigmatic young man clutching a towel around one arm. The youth had told Captain Trevor that he was a college student looking to do some research on the Marquesa Keys, 45 miles west of Key West.

Two hours after the Dream Girl put to sea, Key West police were called to the Royal Palm Motel, on North Roosevelt Boulevard, in response to a troubling discovery. A hotel guest named Roger

Foster had neglected to turn in his key by the 3 p.m. check-out deadline. The hotel manager had used his own pass key to open the door to Foster's room, but found it empty, save for the double bed – which was soaked with blood. He called police, who arrived on the scene a short time later.

A search of Foster's room produced several cryptic clues.

Chief among them was an apparent suicide note retrieved from a wastebasket. "I think I'm insane," it read in part. "Do not publicize my death … be careful when you tell my father because he has a bad heart."

The cops also found a box containing a marine compass, and nautical charts of the Marquesas and the islands of the Dry Tortugas.

The clues were puzzling and the police weren't yet sure that a crime had been committed.

But several hours later, a series of events would help the cops piece together the details of a senseless – yet sensational – crime.

By 6 p.m. that day, the Dream Girl had failed to return to port. It would later be revealed that around this time the vessel had been spotted by a local fisherman heading south at top speed from the Cosgrove Shoals, about 23 miles southwest of Key West.

By 7 p.m., the Coast Guard had received a mysterious "May Day" transmission from an unidentified craft. "There's a dying man aboard," was all the Coasties could decipher from the male voice on the garbled radio message.

At the time of the crime...

In 1963, Key West Police Chief George Gomez was charged with public drunkenness, following an incident in Miami. One week later, he was suspended from his duties. He paid a fine to settle the embarrassing infraction, and resigned from the force early in 1964.

By now, a 95-foot patrol boat, 40-foot rescue craft and a Miami-based Coast Guard patrol plane were searching a 400-square-mile area bounded by the Tortugas, the Marquesas, and Key West.

At some point during the hunt a second, chilling message was broadcast over the marine rescue frequency. "Be careful when you come alongside," the same male voice said. "I have killed two people."

By the next day, April 12, the search was over.

Following a report of an aerial sighting of the Dream Girl by the patrol plane, the 95-foot cutter, captained by commanding officer C.A. Strand intercepted the charter boat drifting less than 20 miles north of the Cuban coast.

Heavily armed Coast Guardsmen boarded the vessel and whisked its sole passenger, a young man wearing a blood-stained T-shirt and chinos, aboard the cutter.

Now a prisoner, the dehydrated, disheveled Foster was locked in a small room for the journey back to Key West. En route, Foster admitted to Chief Petty Officer C.G. Blair, who stood watch over him with a .45 caliber pistol, that he had knifed the Trevors to death and "thrown the bodies overboard, off the Marquesas Keys."

Behind the cutter, the Dream Girl bobbed in the wake of the larger boat during its tow back to its home port, a silent, blood-spattered sentinel to a ghastly and violent double murder.

• • •

Seventeen-year-old Roger Foster was not your typical high school senior.

Though the Griffin, Georgia native was an enthusiastic member of his varsity football team, had a steady girl and was considered bright by his teachers, mother and physician father, Foster clearly had problems.

Politically active beyond his years, Foster strongly disliked the newly installed Cuban dictator Fidel Castro and had tried to start up an anti-communist club at school. This venture failed due to a lack of interest. Not long after, he injured his knee playing football, relegating him to the sidelines and derailing his plans to join the school track team.

In early 1961, Foster's parents had been concerned enough with their son that they took him to see a psychologist in nearby Atlanta. But the shrink sent Foster packing, stating that he could find nothing seriously wrong with the boy.

By early April of 1963, Foster's mental problems were about to boil over – with disastrous consequences.

Just two months before he was due to graduate with honors from Griffin High, Foster got into a fight with his father followed by a spat with his sweetheart.

Despondent, he told his mother that he expected to be late getting in, then climbed into his father's car and began driving south.

His mind churning with irrational thoughts of suicide and political revolution, Foster arrived in Key West on or around the ninth of April, and checked himself into the Royal Palm.

Feeling like a "Viking warrior," as he would later tell a court psychiatrist, he made an unsuccessful attempt to travel to Cuba in a stolen rowboat to "join the Communist Party and to kill Fidel Castro to cause world disorder."

Seeing the folly of his plan, he returned to his hotel room, slashed his left wrist and then fell asleep on his bloody bed.

Waking the next day and realizing he was sill alive, Foster bandaged his injured wrist and then wandered down to the charter boat dock, where he encountered the Trevors. He chartered the Dream Girl and a short time later, the ill-fated captain and his son cast off from the Garrison Bight dock for the last time.

• • •

Around 10:30 a.m. on April 13 as a large crowd gathered on the city fishing pier, the Coast Guard cutter, carrying the still blood-streaked Foster, pulled into port and was quickly boarded by Sheriff Henry Haskins and his men. The deputies and FBI agents then escorted the handcuffed suspect to a waiting car.

Photo courtesy of Monroe County Public Library

The blood-soaked Dream Girl is towed past the city fishing pier, now known as Mallory Square, on the morning of April 13, 1963.

Authorities wasted no time getting to the bottom of what had happened to the Trevors in the hours after the Dream Girl motored out of the City Marina.

Showing no remorse, Foster explained to the police how he had attacked and stabbed both Trevors to death about a mile south of the Marquesas and then tossed their bodies overboard. He offered no explanation for his actions, but said he had hoped to be sentenced to death for the killings so that the electric chair would succeed where his suicide attempt had failed. Later that day, as he was arraigned before Peace Justice Edelmiro Morales, Foster signaled that he understood his rights and the charges against him before entering a guilty plea to the two charges of first-degree murder.

As vessels from the State Conservation Department, the Coast Guard and the Key West Charter Boat Association searched in vain for the bodies of Douglas and Edward Trevor, the wheels of justice

Photo courtesy of Monroe County Public Library

Roger Foster is escorted from the Coast Guard cutter by Sheriff Henry Haskins, at right.

began turning. By late April, Foster's newly hired lawyer Henry Carr, of Miami, declared his intention to have his client declared insane and unable to stand trial. For his part, Foster claimed to be "as rational as anybody," and ready to be executed for his crime.

By Oct. 1, however, Carr's insanity defense strategy won the day. Foster was declared unfit to stand trial and was sent to the South Florida State Hospital in Hollywood. He remained there for the next seven years, despite the protestations of a panel of hospital psychiatrists and psychologists, beginning in December of 1966, that he was now "free of insanity" and competent to stand trial. This finding was disputed by Circuit Court Judge Aquilino Lopez, who refused to consent to Foster's release from the hospital to stand trial.

"Both of the Trevors were very kind to me," Foster told a reporter during this time. "The older man helped me bandage my wrist which I had cut in my motel room, and the younger Trevor shared his lunch with me before I killed him. I had no grudge against either of them ... I think I'm sane."

By February of 1970, the mood of the country was hardened by such recent events as the Manson Family's brutal Tate/LaBianca slayings in California and the tide was turning for Foster. A panel of several state hospital doctors pronounced him sane and filed hospital discharge papers and a certificate of mental competency in the circuit court.

Roger Foster's date with justice was fast approaching.

Following Foster's early April arraignment before Judge Lopez in Key West on two charges of first degree murder, Henry Carr, still representing Foster, succeeded in convincing the judge, on July 1, to move the trial to Miami on the grounds that it would be impossible for his client to receive a fair trial in Key West.

Several Trevor family members sat quietly at the rear of the courtroom during the proceedings as Foster inexplicably posed for snapshots with his parents.

On the morning of Jan. 12, 1971, the jury was seated and Foster was led into the Miami courtroom of Circuit Court Judge Raymond Nathan to answer the charges brought against him. Prosecuting Foster was Palm Beach County assistant state attorney David Bludworth, a onetime Monroe County state attorney.

Though the case might have appeared a slam-dunk, given Foster's confession back in '63, victory for Bludworth was far from assured: Since Foster had been judged to have been insane during the commission of the murders, he could technically be found not guilty by a jury, under Florida law.

Things got off to a flying start.

Douglas Trevor's widow Rosalte Trevor was the first to be brought to the witness stand. She indentified Foster as the man who had made the charter arrangements with her husband on the last day she saw him alive. She then began sobbing uncontrollably and had to be led from the stand. As Rosalte Trevor passed the jury box, she stopped and pleaded with the six-man, six-woman jury.

"Help me," she said. "Please help me."

Judge Nathan rejected Carr's subsequent motion for a mistrial, but did instruct the jury to disregard Rosalte's remark.

The next day, the courtroom heard damning testimony from Coast Guardsmen who had been present during Foster's capture. They recounted the gory scene, right down to Foster's confession.

Monroe County Sheriff "Bobby" Brown, who had been chief criminal investigator at the time of the murders, provided key testimony, and recalled the detailed confession Foster had made to him in those pre-Miranda warning times.

But it was Dr. Albert Jazzlow who offered the grimmest testimony of the trial as he spoke in Foster's defense. On Jan. 14, the Miami psychiatrist, who had examined Foster a week after the slayings, recounted Foster's admission that he had hit the senior Trevor over the head with a flashlight, and then stabbed him with a long-bladed fishing knife. As the younger Trevor rushed to his father's aid, Foster said, he had stabbed him, too; he then stood over the men as they lay dying on the deck of the Dream Girl.

"Don't stab me anymore," were Douglas Trevor's last words to Foster, according to Dr. Jazzlow.

Foster then dumped the bodies into the ocean and steered a course to Cuba.

Sitting behind him in the visitor's gallery, Foster's parents showed no emotion as Jazzlow pronounced their son "insane at the time of the commission of the crime."

Before leaving the stand, the doctor recalled one more thing Foster had told him during their initial contact:

"Life isn't worth much."

It took the jury just five hours to reach its verdict.

At 11 p.m. on Jan. 16, the foreman announced to Judge Nathan that they had found Foster guilty of second-degree murder in the slaying of Douglas Trevor, and Foster was lead from the courtroom to begin serving a life sentence.

Six years later, Bludworth was back for more.

At the behest of Govenor Reubin Askew, Bludworth, by now

the state attorney for Palm Beach County, announced his intention to prosecute Foster for the murder of Edward Trevor. Predictably, Foster, this time defending himself with the aid of a public defender, filed a change of venue motion to have the trial moved outside of Monroe County.

The trial moved to the Miami courtroom of Dade County Chief Criminal Judge Gene Williams, and began in early April of 1977. Once again Sheriff Brown's testimony was all Bludworth needed.

Given the admission of Foster's confession at his previous trial, establishing his guilt in the Edward Trevor case was a mere formality.

Just after lunch on the first day of the trial the court found Foster guilty of second-degree murder.

He was sentenced to an additional 14 years, to run concurrently with his life sentence. One of the longest-running cases in Monroe County history was finally closed.

LEAP OF FAITH:

Possibly the strangest suicide in Key West was that of prominent local lawyer, Fred Butner, who jumped to his death from the 7th floor observatory of the La Concha hotel on Duval Street one day in early October, 1992. In his pockets, police found cash, two notes implicating his secretary in attempts to extort money from him, and a tape recorder. On the tape, Butner appeared to be discussing the woman's demands for hush money with her. At the end of the conversation, the tape captured Butner falling from the building. Police decided the tape was a fake and Butner had staged the stunt to frame his secretary for his death. She was never charged.

Photo by roboneal.com

The Hidden Evil on Big Pine Key

In the late 1980s, someone decided to use the Middle Keys as their own private stalking ground. Nearly 20 years later, the victims' families are still waiting for justice …

Beautiful, tranquil and laid-back, Big Pine Key, in the Middle Keys, is known more for its elfin key deer, alligator-filled "Blue Hole," and 35 mph nightime speed limit than for much else.

Besides the deer, its residents are mostly aging artists and environmental activists. In counterpoint are their pro-development neighbors, agitated that the land they bought to build on years ago has evolved into key deer "habitat," and is now off-limits to construction.

No matter.

For all its drawbacks, the island is largely free of many of the chronic problems residents of large urban areas face. This is what led many people to move to the rural Keys in the first place: It's quiet – except for the Navy jets around Boca Chica – it's safe and most everyone knows each other.

But in the spring of 1988 the idyllic atmosphere of Big Pine Key was rocked by the news that a local woman in her early thirties had been attacked, raped and left for dead. No Name Key, just off Big Pine, had been used before as a dumping ground for a murder victim from Big Coppitt Key, 20 miles to the south. But this was a neighbor who had been brutalized and it jolted a lot of people.

Other incidents followed and soon authorities were investigating three murdered females, as well as the rape, within a year. Women from Little Torch Key through Big Pine were arming themselves with guns and mace worrying that rumors of a satanic cult performing ritual killings were true.

Authorities refused to rule out the possibility, but were frustrated enough with their progress on the cases to admit they hadn't ruled out Martians either.

It appeared, by the barbaric nature of the crimes, that a serial killer, who was more monster than man, was stalking the female citizens of the Middle Keys on the lonely moonlit roads that crisscross the archipelago.

Let's examine what happened in those dark days in '88 and '89, when the sky really seemed to be falling on the Middle Keys.

The first victim had been walking alone near the intersection of Hibiscus Lane and County Road when she said she was attacked, beaten and raped by a "slender white man with shoulder-length, brownish-blond curly hair," the Key West Citizen revealed on July 30, 1989. Even the hardened sheriff's deputies on the scene were shocked at the viciousness of the attack, which left the woman with a broken jaw and multiple lacerations. Plastic surgery was needed to reconstruct her face.

The Monroe County Sheriff's Office was investigating the crime as an isolated incident when the first gruesome murder took place.

The victim was a 4-year-old girl named Patty Lanza who wandered away from a Little Torch Key Fourth of July party and was later found sexually assaulted and murdered. A suspect was charged with false imprisonment of a child under the age of 13 after one of the murdered girl's friends told police she saw a man walk off into the brush with her. But nobody saw the actual assault and the cops had to let the man go.

Two weeks into December, the unthinkable happened – again. A woman in her early 20s was found raped, beaten and murdered on No Name Key. Her jaw had been broken and detectives said they thought she had been dragged behind a car for about half a mile before her death.

At the time of the crime...

In 1989, Key West police detectives Steve Hammers and Robert Allen were shot and wounded in Bahama Village while attempting to arrest a suspect in a narcotics case. The perpetrator, who was shot five times in the buttocks during the incident, bled to death. Hammers and Allen both survived and eventually returned to active duty.

On Dec. 21, the victim was identified as Lisa Sanders, 20, a new resident of Big Pine Key who moved there from Michigan following a lengthy and successful fight with leukemia.

She and a small group of friends had gone to a rowdy outdoor party on No Name Key. Shortly after arriving, Sanders told her friends she wanted to leave. They weren't ready to go yet, so she set off on foot. When Sanders didn't show up at home the next morning, her worried parents called police, who later confirmed their worst fears.

"Since Saturday, 10 detectives have put in excess of 800 man hours in the case," Detective Sgt. Jerry Powell said at a Dec. 22 news conference, held to announce a $5,000 reward for information.

Sheriff-Elect J. Allison DeFoor II also waded into the fray, declaring, "I will request the department prepare plans for aggressive action to deal with the spirit of lawlessness in the area between Big Coppitt and Big Pine Keys."

Meanwhile, Marilyn Sanders sold her daughter's trailer and used the money to start a reward fund of her own. "No young woman should be out alone, day or night walking anywhere," she told the Citizen.

By the end of January, 1989, the cops still had no progress to report, despite questioning more than 100 people.

"The cases will remain active until we find out who did it," Sheriff's Spokeswoman Becky Herrin said. "We don't close homicides."

Seven months later, on July 19, an Ohio family fishing in the South Pine Channel reeled in the disfigured body of Sherry Perisho, 38. Her face, throat and abdomen had been slashed. Locals called Perisho "Rainmaker," since the latter-day hippie often claimed to be able to cause rain to fall. She had been known to sleep in a dinghy under a bridge and was probably doing just that at the time of her murder.

This killing caused an uproar.

Wild rumors about a satanic drug-and-ritual murder cult began to circulate around the small community. The sheriff's office had admitted that it was "in the process of consulting with some out-of-state experts on satanic rituals," and it announced the creation of a Big Pine cross-jurisdictional task force. This included officers from the Florida Department of Law Enforcement, the State Attorney's Office, the sheriff's Special Operations Division and others. Employees of local utility companies, who often worked in areas where the attacks occurred, were given training courses by the police to make them more alert to questionable activities.

On Aug. 1, police shocked the community further when they revealed that the bodies of Sanders and Perisho were missing their hearts at the time they were found. DeFoor admitted his deputies also found "satanic markings" at one of the crime scenes and that he was aware of satanic groups, presumably in the area.

On Aug. 12, the Miami Herald reported that police had linked a man to two of the killings. Michael Bologna, 35, of Big Pine Key had been with Deborah Lanza, Patty's mother, at the Big Torch Key party where Patty had disappeared. He'd also dated Perisho for a while, but police later admitted he wasn't much of a suspect and that he had cooperated with them in every way. His landlord called him "a fine young man," adding that "the fact that he knew the two girls is just one of those coincidences."

Members of the Lanza and Sanders families became convinced that there was a satanic cult involved in both murders. Police responded that they weren't even sure the murders were related, though they allowed that they had found a five-sided pentagram star design on the road near Sanders' body.

A Marathon church employee named Rhonda Poor admitted she counseled "six or seven" young recovering cultists. She said they told her they "use girls for ritual offerings on altars," lying on slabs. "One boy said he had to take a large live animal, kill it, and drink the blood," she said.

Police continued to state that they had no way to link the cases, but Dade County Medical Examiner Joseph Davis, who assisted in the investigation, believed otherwise. "Psychopathic killers frequently use different ways to kill different people," he said. "There's a very compelling link in these murders: Geography and time."

Two years went by without a break in the cases or another seemingly related murder taking place. Residents of the Lower and Middle Keys held their collective breath.

Then, the day after Valentine's Day, 1991, windsurfers found the naked body of another young woman in the Bahia Honda State Park. She had been beaten, raped and strangled with her own bikini top. The woman was a Jane Doe with no identification, who had reportedly been seen hitchhiking from Stock Island at Mile Marker 4, up to the park at Mile Marker 35. Bahia Honda is just north of Big Pine Key, so investigators hesitated to link the murder to the ongoing investigation of the Big Pine cases. However, the killing was soon added to the "unsolved" list as no clues or leads materialized.

In the years since the first rape turned the community upside down, no charges have been filed in relation to any of the crimes.

But in the fall of 2004, authorities in Seminole County, Florida, reported a grisly discovery with an eerie Keys connection: On Sept. 15 of that year, Michelle Jones, 38, was found murdered in the bedroom of her Altamonte Springs home. Her head and leg had been severed and her heart had been ripped out of her chest. Also found at the gruesome scene was the body of her aunt Teresa Brandt, who had been stabbed to death, and that of her uncle, Carl "Charlie" Brandt, who was found hanging from a sheet in the garage. The Brandts were both longtime residents of Big Pine Key who had sought refuge at Jones' home from Hurricane Ivan, which was then bearing down on the Keys.

Further, Carl Brandt, who lived near the spot where Sherry Perisho had turned up dead in 1989, had a violent history, having shot his parents – killing his mother – when he was a 13-year-old in Fort Wayne, Indiana. He hadn't been indicted for the crimes at the time, due to his age.

As a result of these latest developments, authorities expanded their investigation of the double-murder/suicide to include Perisho's murder and the killing of another woman in Miami, in 1995.

In early May 2006, the Monroe County Sheriff's Office finally concluded, after more than 100 interviews and 110 pieces of evidence collected, that Brandt had, in fact, murdered Sherry Perisho. At press time, there was no word as to whether authorities suspected his involvement in any of the other killings that took place in the late 1980s and early '90s, in the Middle Keys.

The tragic cases still rank among the great unsolved mysteries of the Keys.

HELP WANTED:

A cold case squad made up of Monroe County Sheriff's Office deputies continues to look into the Big Pine murder cases. They welcome any information on the crimes at 1-800-346-TIPS.

Photo courtesy of Monroe County Public Library

The Key West Depot, of the East Coast Railway, was a transfer point for steamship passengers traveling between Cuba and Key West.

Prohibition and the Politician

Caught smuggling booze into Key West from Cuba, this Prohibition-friendly congressman was put in a bind. Like a true politician, he decided to pass the buck…

Few issues have divided Americans as bitterly as Prohibition did in the 1910s and '20s. On one side were those who felt that alcohol led to moral rot, an unproductive workforce and broken families. Opposing them were those who felt that the 18th Amendment to the Constitution, which came into effect on Jan. 16, 1920, prohibiting the "manufacture, transportation, sale and possession of alcoholic beverages in the United States," was an unwarranted federal intrusion into the lives of citizens. These opponents of Prohibition predicted that it would fail and serve only to breed violent organized crime. The latter argument won out and Prohibition was repealed in 1933.

But during that 13-year dry spell, most Key Westers were as enthusiastic about Prohibition as they had been about being a Union town during the Civil War. Given the island's proximity to Cuba and the Bahamas, and its somewhat roguish past, Key West stayed soaking wet during this period and profited from the alcohol-inspired boom in Cuba tourism.

The G-men did come down to Key West to try to put a stop to the rum-running and illegal gin joints, but their efforts never amounted to much. Their use of railroad passes tipped off the train conductors, who made sure that word of their mission reached the right ears in the Southernmost City.

Garden of Roses bar owner Pena Morales described the routine to historians Wright and Joan Langley in their 1982 book *Key West Images of the Past*:

"The conductors would signal the station master. He, in turn, would call up Key West and tell the station master here that a bunch of government raiders were on the way down the Keys. The station master at this end would get a hold of chauffeurs and taxi men and they would spread the word. By the time the Feds got here, the liquor supply would be safely hidden."

It's difficult to imagine a better example of Key Westers' legendary dismissive attitudes regarding the far-off federal government and its meddlesome laws.

One visitor to Key West who most definitely did agree with Prohibition was Congressman Magne Alfred Michaelson who passed through town from Cuba on his way to New York City on Jan. 3, 1928. Campaigning for re-election to his Seventh Illinois District seat in the fall of 1928, Michaelson, a Republican, secured the backing of the Anti-Saloon League. Following his successful re-election bid to the House of Representatives, he voted for the "Jones Bills," dubbed the "Five and Ten" laws, which toughened penalties for violators of the Prohibition laws.

For these reasons, Key West residents were understandably shocked to learn that, on March 29, 1929, the good congressman – who had been expedited through the port of Key West, without his luggage being searched – had been indicted for importing booze into the country during his pre-election swing through Key West. Though the federal grand jury had indicted Michaelson in October of '28, the situation had somehow been kept secret until the lawmaker had been safely re-elected – with the help of the Anti-Saloon League, and its supporters.

With the cat out of the bag, details of the charges began to emerge.

The liquor, Prohibition Administrator W.T. Day said, had been discovered in two of Michaelson's six trunks at a train station in Jacksonville, Florida. One of the bags had sprung a leak, alerting sharp-eyed baggage handlers to its contents. They called the coppers, who opened the luggage to find 12 quarts and a 1 gallon demi-john of liquor, as well as a jug of some sort of alcoholic cordial.

At the time of the crime...

In 1928, the speakeasies of Key West were gifted with one of their best customers, when author Ernest Hemingway moved to the Island City with his wife, Pauline.

The bags were seized and the Feds were notified.

On March 29, a warrant was issued for Michaelson's arrest. He surrendered to U.S. Marshals at the federal building in Chicago and posted a $2,000 bond. Waiving a preliminary hearing, he agreed to voluntarily come to Key West and face trial on May 6, but strongly denied all the charges against him. His bond posted, Michaelson left the building escorted by two federal officers "assigned to him to prevent reporters from questioning him, or photographers from taking pictures," the Associated Press reported.

Michaelson's arrest had been delayed "in abeyance," it was said, until Congress adjourned as members are technically immune from prosecution from all but the most serious crimes, while that August body is in session. And the delay in prosecuting the honorable member since Congress took its break was nothing more than the result of a heavy backlog of cases, according to George Johnson, the United States district attorney for Chicago.

As promised, Congressman Michaelson appeared before Judge Halsted Ritter and a jury in the Key West courtroom. He and his attorney, H.H. Taylor, faced the prosecutorial team of acting District Attorney William Hughes and N. J. Morrison, the special assistant to the attorney general of the United States.

If convicted of the charges against him, Michaelson would become, ironically, the first high profile defendant to face the new, higher sentencing guidelines prescribed under the Jones Bills he had supported the year before.

But it was not to be.

One can almost imagine the gasps of disbelief and Judge Ritter banging his gavel for order as Michaelson dropped his bombshell in the crowded courtroom: I didn't do it...my brother-in-law did.

Indeed, Walter Gramm, who had accompanied Michaelson on his fateful Cuba trip back in January of '28, told the court that the liquor was his and that he had smuggled it into the country in the unsuspecting congressman's luggage.

Given his testimony, the jury had little choice but to acquit

Michaelson, which they did, in the early morning of May 9.

An exasperated Hughes immediately indicted Gramm, who was led away mumbling something about being sorry, to post bond of $2,000 – the same amount Michaelson had just had returned to him upon his acquittal.

Gramm's case was moved to Jacksonville, leaving Michaelson sitting pretty in Chicago and Hughes with egg on his face.

Gramm was the " 'fall guy' for Michaelson, who came here to take his brother-in-law's blame upon himself," Hughes griped to the Associated Press.

But Congressman Michaelson did not survive the incident unscathed: The publicity dogged him like a stubborn hangover and the following year, the GOP refused to renominate him to the seat he had held since 1921.

He died on Oct. 26, 1949, in Chicago.

Gone…but not forgotten.

A SMUGGLER GOES OVERBOARD:

On Oct. 30, 1930, the Key West Citizen reported that a Coast Guard patrol boat had shot and killed notorious rumrunner Willie "Twisteye" Demeritt during a confrontation in Hawks Channel. Members of the smuggler's captured crew told police that Demeritt had been shot at close range, and fell overboard and drowned. But authorities doubted this story, as Demeritt had disappeared overboard before, then reappeared in Cuba. Sure enough, this time he turned up safe and sound, and lived to smuggle more rum from Cuba to Key West.

Photo courtesy of Monroe County Public Library

The Boca Chica Lounge, circa 1977.

Say Hello to My Little Friend ...

Late-night parties at the Boca Chica Lounge often turned ugly. During one late-night bender, things turned murderous ...

Driven by growing demand and fueled by a subsequent increase in supply, the smuggling of cocaine into South Florida picked up speed throughout the 1970s. By the early '80s, it accelerated into overdrive and then spun wildly out of control.

Drug smuggling "started out as an Anglo adventure, and became a Cuban business," former Key West writer Tom McGuane, author of *92 Degrees in the Shade*, has said.

In the spring of 1980, Cuban President Fidel Castro opened the port of Mariel, near Havana and announced that any Cubans who wished to flee the country would be permitted to do so. A flotilla of small American boats, many of them owned or captained by Cuban Americans, arrived at Mariel to pick up friends and relatives and return with them to the United States. The vast majority of these 125,000 refugees were honest citizens who went on to build productive new lives in their adopted country. But the Mariel Boatlift had its dark side as well, as Castro emptied the worst elements from his jails and forced the American captains to take these nearly 20,000 hardcore criminals back to the U.S. with them.

This watershed event gave a shot in the arm to organized crime in South Florida, transforming the region – and its smuggling trade – almost overnight.

In fact, most of the "Cuban crime wave" depicted in Martin Scorsese's classic 1983 film "Scarface" ended up in the Miami area, but the Keys also saw their share of harrowing, drug-related situations in those early days of the "cocaine cowboys."

One such incident took place in the early morning of April 28, 1984 at the Boca Chica Lounge on Stock Island.

Located just across the Cow Key Bridge from Key West, the landmark watering hole had been in business since the 1950s. Since it was technically outside of town, it was not subject to Key West liquor laws, and stayed open well past 4 a.m., when bars just across the bridge had to close up.

"Although it had a reputation as a 'knife and gun' club, the majority of its patrons were area bartenders, servers and late-night employees from a wide range of local businesses and a few 'in the know' tourists," one-time owner Rick Berard wrote in the Key West Morning Star newspaper in 2000. But, "When something bad happened, it was usually really bad."

At 4:35 a.m. on April 28, the joint was hopping and Berard went into the bar's office to get a roll of quarters for one of his waitresses. While inside, he heard three pops that sounded like firecrackers going off.

Thinking a prankster was playing a joke in the barroom, Berard opened the office door and peered out. The lounge, which had been full when he walked into the office, was now deserted.

Or so it seemed.

As he walked out into the bar, Berard realized that his customers were all on the floor, hiding behind tables, chairs, and anything else they could use as a shield. In the rear of the bar, lying by the pool tables, a figure lay sprawled on the floor.

Berard ran over to examine the man, noticed a small red dot in the front of his white T-shirt, and realized he had been shot.

Shortly afterwards, the police and an ambulance arrived to take the victim, later identified as Juan Prat Valdez, 44, of Key West, to the hospital, where he was pronounced dead.

As he talked to the officers at the scene, Berard realized that Valdez wasn't the only fatality in the incident. Just down the road, minutes after the shooting, two other Latin males walking across

At the time of the crime...

In the spring of 1985, federal drug indictments were served upon a number of high-ranking Key West police officers, public officials and civilians during the infamous "Bubba Bust."

the Cow Key Bridge towards Key West had been run over and killed by a champagne pink 1975 Cadillac, which then missed the turn at the traffic triangle and ended up in the pool at the Quality Inn on North Roosevelt Boulevard. The car matched the description of one that had been seen leaving the Boca Chica parking lot immediately after the initial shooting. There were bullet holes in its windshield, but no driver was discovered inside.

By April 30, the two hit-and-run victims were identified as Oviedo E. Torres, 24, and Cibio P. Acevedo, 26. Like Valdez, both Torres and Acevedo were Marielitos living in Key West, and both were allegedly active in the drug trade.

Not long afterwards, a fourth body, possibly that of the driver of the Caddy, was found under Cow Key Bridge near the Quality Inn.

Accounts of what really happened that morning varied, but Berard said the cops thought Torres and Acevedo had been dropped off in front of the Boca Chica Lounge to shoot Valdez and then ran out the back door expecting to find their getaway car waiting for them. It wasn't, so the pair ran off on foot towards Key West. Then a friend, relative, or business associate of Valdez came after them and ran them both over.

'SQUARE GROUPER' SCOOPER:

During the heyday of pot smuggling in the Keys, the contraband bales were often referred to as "square grouper" as they were often found floating in the water or washed up on beaches. In June of 1978, a Key West teenager who foolishly stole some pot bales from local smugglers, told police he was abducted and taken to a house on the mainland. His head was held to a hot barbecue grill and he was given an unwanted and terrifying haircut with a chainsaw.

Presumably, the assassins had squeezed off a couple of shots before they were killed, hitting the windshield of the Cadillac. It's possible that they hit the driver, who then abandoned the car and fled the scene, before succumbing to his injuries beneath the bridge.

It's also possible that the truth about what happened will never be known.

The witnesses appear to have all killed each other.

Say Hello to my Little Friend

Photo courtesy of Monroe County Public Library

The Sociedad Cuba, or Cuban Club, where the Navy held its 'smoker' benefits, in the 1950s.

The Stag Smoker Sex Scandal

Think your last fundraising party was the wildest one ever? Read this story, and think again…

Many people love a good ol' sex scandal. Especially when the scandal involves politicians.

Yet public revelations of the sexual shenanigans of prominent people have always been few and far between in the Keys. Or at least they were in days past when people made a point of minding their own business.

Open prostitution flourished right up until the early 1940s in Bahama Village, with brothels operating in buildings such as the one currently occupied by the landmark Blue Heaven restaurant at Thomas and Petronia streets. "Mom's Tea Room," also located in Bahama Village, was another favorite fleshpot of civilians and members of the armed forces. It relocated to a building on Stock Island, where Boyd's Campground stands today, after the Navy pressured the Key West city government to shut down the Bahama Village bordellos in 1942.

At any rate, you weren't going to read about these goings-on in the locally owned and operated Key West press, which avoided such embarrassing disclosures of impropriety. Not that it mattered. Everybody in this small town knew everybody else's business, anyway. They just didn't talk about it in public.

As for the officers and sailors of the United States Navy, they were literally a commanding presence in town in those days and constituted a good chunk of the clientele of the houses of ill repute. But, as everybody knows, military courts can operate independently from the civilian process and the media, often under strict rules of secrecy.

For these reasons, Key West's greatest sex scandal was an open, yet unreported secret for about four months, before all the national attention it received made it impossible for the local papers to ignore it any longer.

Here's how it all went down:

By the early 1950s, the Navy and their dependents numbered some 20,000 personnel stationed at the bases in Key West and Boca Chica. And each year, local Navy brass organized "stag smoker" parties for the benefit of the Navy's Charity Carnival. These smoky, boozy benders, staged so the men could blow off a little steam, were raucous affairs. The smoker held on Feb. 2, 1953* was no exception.

What was exceptional about the party, held at the Cuban Club on upper Duval Street, was the evening's entertainment. In addition to the usual food, booze and spicy stag films, organizers had procured "talent" from Mom's Tea Room to put on a stage show. And at some point in the evening, the show turned participatory, with at least three Navy men jumping onstage to avail themselves of the opportunity to take the show one step further.

It was shocking; it was scandalous. But this was Key West in the 1950s, so the incident was forgotten.

Unfortunately for the benefit's organizers, someone present in the mixed Navy/civilian crowd squealed to the national press that the Navy had organized a live sex show in Key West and that several prominent public figures had been on hand for the spectacle. It later turned out that a Navy chaplain named Greer S. Imbrie had been the whistleblower.

By June, the nationally syndicated columnist Drew Pearson had blown the lid off the smokers in his "Washington Merry-Go-Round" column, which was carried by the Miami Herald. In his salacious piece, Pearson said that Key West Mayor C.B. Harvey, City Commissioner John Carbonell, County Judge Raymond R. Lord, Key West Police Chief Joseph Kemp, former city manager Dave King, and Gerald Guthrie, principal of Sue Moore School in Marathon, had all been in attendance at the sordid affair. Harvey, Pearson said, had even been sitting up near the front of the stage, in what he termed the "bald headed row."

Shortly after the column's publication, Harvey announced that he was going to sue Pearson and the Herald for libel, and that was

* A second, equally sensational smoker was held a week later.

enough to draw the Key West Citizen into the fray. On the front page of the June 29, 1953 edition, the paper acknowledged for the first time what had happened at the party and stated that several Navy men had already been convicted for their roles in the affair on charges ranging from "conduct of a nature to bring discredit to the armed forces," to sodomy. One sailor, Airman Robert W. Spangenberg, of Naval Air Station Key West received a "bad conduct discharge" and a year in the slammer.

Another man, Lt. Comdr. Gerry McDaniel, who was said to have arranged the smoker, faced court martial on charges of conspiracy, willful disobedience of a lawful order and conduct unbecoming an officer and a gentleman. If convicted, the 28-year Navy man, who had just three months to go until retirement, faced dismissal from the Navy and the loss of his retirement benefits.

For their part, the other prominent Key Westers ducked for cover. Commissioner Carbonell flat-out denied being present, while Police Chief Kemp, former city manager King, and Principal Guthrie admitted they had been there, but said they had left before the lewd acts occurred.

"I certainly didn't see any wrestling," King said, alluding to allegations that a female entertainer had invited audience members on stage to wrestle with her. Judge Lord was "on vacation and could not be reached," though he later admitted to being at the first smoker, but leaving before it got out of hand.

An indignant American Legion official, Vance Stirrup, denied that the Legion loaned the Navy the stag films shown at the smoker, disputing another of Pearson's charges. "We don't keep a supply of them here," he said.

But in a statement that was extremely revealing about the protective nature of the community towards its own, City Commissioner Jack Delaney declared that the city couldn't "ignore the situation any longer … now that this thing has been brought out in the open in newspapers all over the nation."

This sudden public stinkbomb which, by now, had been discussed on the floor of the U.S. Congress, was actually the Navy's problem as it was their event, held in a hall they had rented. In Key West, the Navy buck stopped with Admiral Irving T. Duke, who was out of town when the revelations were made public. Duke had just received transfer orders to a position in the Pacific command, but denied that the stag smoker had anything to do with the move, which he called "routine."

On June 30, the day after the Citizen's first article appeared, the paper announced that Lt. Comdr. McDaniel was to be tried on the three charges against him at the Sixth Naval District Headquarters in Charleston, S.C. He was expected to counter with allegations, first brought up in Pearson's column, that he had been illegally detained by the Navy, without being charged, for 40 days from March 6 to April 16. The Navy denied that he had been held in violation of the law. And in the most graphic statement yet on the smokers, Citizen reporter Jim Cobb stated that the two parties had "reportedly degenerated into sex orgies."

McDaniel's trial, set to take place on July 14, was shaping up as a lurid affair, to say the least. Two of the other Navy men in the court's sights had already pleaded guilty to the charges against them and thrown themselves on the court's mercy. Two other still faced trial. McDaniel, though, remained defiant. He was fighting for his career and future economic security against a body that clearly wanted this case with all its attendant publicity to go away. It was even rumored that

At the time of the crime...

In late 1953 and early 1954, allegations of corruption led to a grand jury probe of the Key West Police Department. The investigation went nowhere.

"Sheila," the dark-haired showgirl who had performed the lewd acts onstage at the first smoker would testify at the trial. Both Collier's and Life magazines had reporters covering the sensational courtroom drama, which, in a surprise move, was then sent to the Pensacola Naval Air Station.

Meanwhile, McDaniel received some welcome moral support from members of the American Legion in his hometown of Gulfport, Mississippi. The members declared him innocent and called him a victim of a cover-up attempt by Navy higher-ups to hide their own guilt in the affair. By Aug. 2, the Citizen reported that his trial had been postponed yet again. Speculation began to mount that he might never actually be tried as his testimony could be damaging to high-ranking Navy as well as Key West and Monroe County officials. The trials of McDaniel's two other colleagues were moved to Key West and the orders transferring Rear Admiral Irving T. Duke and Naval Station Legal Officer Lt. Cmdr. Ben Berry were cancelled.

Something, clearly, was brewing.

At a secrecy-shrouded trial on Aug. 13 in Key West, Boatswain's Mate 2nd Class Raymond R. Robinson was found guilty by a Summary Court Martial on two charges relating to the procurement of "Sheila" from Mom's Tea Room – which was out-of-bounds to Navy men – for the smoker. His fellow defendant, Seaman Apprentice Victor R. Cramer, had testified against him after Rear Admiral Duke granted him immunity from prosecution in exchange for his cooperation.

Cramer, it seems, had been in possession of the tickets and proceeds on the night of the first smoker. He told the court that he gave $100 from the receipts to Howard E. MacDonald, a civilian clerk at the NAS, to "get a girl from Mom's to put on an act." Later on in the evening, he said, he saw the scantily clad "Sheila," Rose Rabin, aka "Mom," from the Tea Room, and Robinson, walking towards the Cuban Club stage. What followed, he said was a "shocking performance," which he only glanced at.

To recap, Robinson, who had a spotless eight-year Navy record, received the first blot on his name, a $100 fine and a 30-day restriction to base. Cramer, who admitted he gave Navy fundraising money and instructions to hire a hooker, got a reprieve.

Then, the whole affair appeared to peter out.

On Aug. 15 the Navy announced that "a general order to clear all enlisted men connected with the case and reprimand all officers" was in the offing, an action that would free at least one man from jail and remand the fines doled out to the other defendants in the case. Navy sources also said that McDaniel had been given a severe reprimand and forfeiture of pay – basically a slap on the wrist – to put an end to this embarrassing scandal. He was also told that he was to be reassigned. A few days later, the Navy dropped all charges against two remaining defendants and it was all over.

For members of the Key West Navy brass, though, things were just heating up.

By early September, the office of Secretary of the Navy Robert A. Anderson announced that it was issuing reprimands to Rear Admiral Duke and Legal Officer Berry, both of whom had since been reassigned, for their mishandling of the investigation. Pentagon sources said Duke and Berry should have convened a formal Naval Board of Inquiry to get to the bottom of what happened as soon as the investigation began. Instead, the two officers held at least two men incommunicado, one of them in a dark cell, and used old-fashioned police methods to get them to confess their misdeeds. Duke and Berry also tried to intimidate one of the men and his wife by telling them that "their lives were in danger," the source said. It'll never be known whether the men were suspected of trying to scapegoat their underlings to cover up the whole mess. But the reprimands put an end to any possibility of upward mobility in their Navy careers.

A postscript: On Jan. 5, 1955, the U.S. Court of Military Appeals ruled that the general court martial in the smoker case may have erred when it discharged a 22-year-old petty officer after convicting him on sodomy charges. The appeals court said that the man had been discharged, apparently and inexplicably, because of a Navy regulation directing the discharge of known homosexuals even though there had been no evidence of homosexuality at the smoker. The court then directed the Navy to take another look at the case and possibly reinstate the sailor if he had been wrongly convicted. The blanket amnesty proclaimed by the Navy two years earlier had, apparently, not been fully carried out. It's unclear from the press reports what happened to the young sailor.

However, this story does have a happy ending. The smokers ended up raising about $70,000, in 1953 dollars, for the Navy charity.

REBIRTH OF A LANDMARK:

The Key West Cuban Club on Duval Street, where the Navy held its rowdy parties, was built in 1917 as a club for the families of immigrant cigar makers from Cuba. Along with the fortunes of the town, it fell into decline in the 1960s and '70s. After being gutted by a fire in the early 1980s, it was restored and now houses luxury rental suites.

Photo courtesy of Monroe County Public Library

Key West Police Officer Clarence K. Till, 1873-1904

The Murder of Clarence Till

Walking a beat in the rough days of Key West's past could be risky. An officer could even get killed . . .

It's hard for many newcomers to the Florida Keys to realize just what a tough town Key West could be back in the late 1800s and early 1900s. Not only did questionable individuals arrive almost daily in the seaport town by way of ships, but locals, too, were often in hot water with the law.

Though gambling, bootlegging and prostitution were technically illegal, these activities flourished in a climate of unofficial tolerance, with conveniently organized arrests occurring on a rotating basis to help fill the city coffers and keep the government happy without inconveniencing – too much – the lawbreakers themselves.

One crime, however, was not tolerated in those wild, woolly days, and that was murder – especially the murder of a peace officer, which is what took place the evening of March 7, 1904.

On that date, a Key West policeman named Clarence K. Till, a former soldier who had arrived in Key West during the Spanish-American War, answered a call involving a drunken disturbance at a downtown coffee shop. The caller, apparently the owner of the establishment, claimed that one of the men involved in the fracas had broken a window in the place. The scene was getting uglier by the minute when Till, 31, arrived and began asking questions.

After a spell, a local man from a prominent family named Herbert "Dutchy" Melbourne, then 24, stepped forward and admitted that he was the one who had broken the window. But when Till attempted to place Melbourne under arrest, he resisted and began hitting Till with his fists. At this point, the drunken crowd joined in grabbing Till's gun and slicing him across his forehead in an apparent attempt to scalp him.

Somehow Till managed to escape from the bloodthirsty mob and hurried to the home of Key West Mayor Benjamin Douglas Trevor to inform him of the situation. Horrified, Trevor armed himself and Till and the pair set out to break up the riot.

But the two men never arrived.

According to newspaper accounts unearthed by Monroe County

Public Library historians Tom and Lynda Hambright, "Dutchy" Melbourne stepped from the shadows on a nearby street and opened fire. The first shot struck Till and he dropped to the pavement without a word. Melbourne then approached the fallen officer and, firing several more shots into his body, shouted "This is an old grudge."

Trevor now returned fire, hitting Melbourne in the arm, whereupon, Melbourne fled the scene. He was arrested the next day at his mother's house by county Sheriff R.F. Hicks and Key West Police Captain Albury and taken to the county jail. On the way over he told the officers how much he regretted not having shot the mayor as well as Till.

The day after the crime, a coroner's jury was convened to hear five days of testimony and concluded on March 13 that, although Melbourne had been the principal figure in the slaying, three other local men – Will Cash, Arthur Sheppard, and George Roberts – also took part and should be charged as accessories. On May 3, the Monroe County grand jury indicted Melbourne for murder and set his trial date for Nov. 23.

During the trial, Melbourne, who was being defended by attorney L.A. Harris, sat expressionless and listened as Mayor Trevor related his version of the incident to Judge J.P. Wall and the assembled jury. On Nov. 26, Melbourne was found guilty of first-degree murder and sentenced to hang.

At the time of the crime...

In 1904, Key West Police Officer Hopkins shot and killed a presumably drunk sailor named "Druro," who attacked him with a fence picket. The officer had been trying to convince the sailor and three of his colleagues to leave the premises, where a number of women resided.

But in June of 1905 this conviction was overturned and Melbourne was ordered released on bail until his retrial. Finally, in November of 1907, after several delays, Melbourne was retried, found guilty of manslaughter, and sentenced to one year in the county jail.

While he was an inmate at the jail, Melbourne was hired out as convict labor to the Key West Fire Department. During the course of this community service, he and several of his fellow workers formed a gang that came to be suspected of carrying out robberies and burning down the old Cortez cigar factory in 1908.

All four men were convicted and sentenced to 13 years in prison, but Dutchy Melbourne escaped on Oct. 21, 1909 and fled to southwest Florida to find work on a farm. Thanks to his well-connected Key West family, the law didn't pursue him there.

Less than a year later, though, his luck finally ran out. Melbourne was murdered by a farm owner who had a habit of killing his employees at the end of the harvest so as not to have to pay them for their labors. And though he's been dead for nearly a century, the scoundrel Melbourne lives on in infamy: His tale was dramatized in famed wilderness writer Peter Matthiessen's quasi-historical 1990 novel *Killing Mister Watson*.

WIDOW'S WALK:

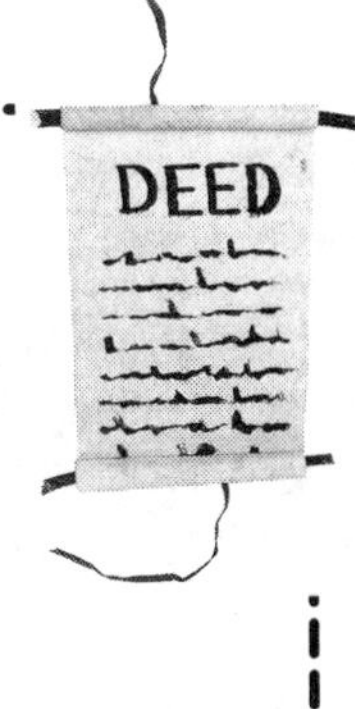

Not long after the shooting of Officer Clarence Till, the Key West City Council took up a collection for his widow and on July 3, 1904 presented her with the deed to a wooden Conch house at 1215 Newton St. Today, Till's name is inscribed (West Wall, Panel 35, Line 20,) on the National Law Enforcement Memorial in Washington D.C., a fitting tribute to the fallen officer.

Photo by roboneal.com

The 801 Bourbon Bar, formerly Big Mama's, at the corner of Duval and Petronia streets.

Wrong Place, Wrong Time

The middle of a violent love triangle is no place to be at the best of times. At its worst, even innocent bystanders are fair game …

All too often, people end up in the wrong place at the wrong time and find themselves on the receiving end of a hail of gunfire. This fate befell a pair of Key West men who paid a high price for their friend's indiscretion one night during the summer of 1976.

Joseph W. Patrick was the owner of both the Raceway Inn bar on Stock Island, and Big Mama's bar at the corner of Duval and Petronia streets, where the 801 Bourbon Bar stands today. On the evening of July 29, 1976 he arrived at the Raceway to hang out with local U.S. Army Sergeant James Alfred Robinson, who was interested in buying Big Mama's from him. As he waited for Robinson, Patrick met up with Kay Klittorp Nielsen, another locally-stationed U.S. Army sergeant. Eventually, Robinson showed up as well, accompanied by Warren Belvin, a friend who came along to advise him on what would be involved with renovating Big Mama's, which had been damaged in a recent fire.

As they talked, Nielsen asked Robinson if he could catch a ride with him when he was finished inspecting Big Mama's. His fellow soldier agreed and the four men piled into Robinson's car and drove to the bar. They looked the place over and then headed down Petronia Street to the Regular Fellows Club for a quick drink.

Half an hour later the party got up to leave, with Robinson and Patrick exiting first. But as they stepped onto the sidewalk, a face that was all too familiar to Robinson appeared across Petronia Street: It was that of Donald "Ducky" Bennett, an employee of the nearby 21 Club, with whom Robinson had been quarreling for weeks over a woman.

A series of shots rang out.

Not far away, Key West Police Sgt. Henry Roberts heard the gunfire and came running, radioing his dispatcher as he raced down Petronia Street. Arriving on the scene, he spotted Bennett walking down the sidewalk and ordered him to stop. Bennett ducked into the 21 Club, so Roberts went inside and placed "Ducky" under arrest. A short time later, he brought his captive outside and shoved him into a squad car.

Around this time, police officer Mike Young showed up and, seeing that Bennett had already been secured, went over to the entrance to Regular Fellows Club to attend to the victims.

On one side of Robinson's car, he found Patrick – who obviously never knew what or who hit him – still alive, but bleeding badly from a gunshot that had gone through his left arm and entered his chest. On the other side was Robinson, who was already dead due to at least one shotgun blast to the back of his head.

Entering Regular Fellows, Young encountered Kay Nielsen, the man who literally was just along for the ride, lying face down and bleeding on the floor of the bar, and also probably dead.

As the squad car containing Bennett pulled away from the curb on the way to the jail, the ambulance pulled up and took Patrick, Robinson and Nielsen to Florida Keys Memorial Hospital.

There, it was discovered that Nielsen and Robinson were, in fact, already dead, Nielsen from two shots to the chest from a .22 caliber rifle and Robinson from six shots from the same gun and a .12 gauge shotgun blast to the back of the head. Patrick, who had been shot once with the .22, hung on for a little while, but eventually died.

At the time of the crime...

In 1975, Key West police officer Norman Alvin Drew became the second officer from the department to die in the line of duty, when he was fatally injured in a crash involving his police motorcycle.

Bennett, who friends said had fought violently with Robinson over the woman they had both been dating, was the obvious suspect in the slayings and had been seen shooting at least one of the men by a woman walking down the street. Held without bail, he was indicted by the Monroe County grand jury a week later for three counts of first-degree murder.

But the State Attorney's office had problems making the charges stick.

For one thing, there really was no motive for the killing of Nielsen and Patrick. Secondly, no witnesses actually saw the whole affair play out.

"As far as premeditation is concerned, we have no cases to get a first-degree verdict," State Attorney Jeff Gautier told visiting Circuit Court Judge Victor Wehle during the trial in April, 1977.

Finally, a deal was struck between the State and Bennett: He would not go to the electric chair, but instead would serve three consecutive life terms in prison.

At least one man involved in this tragic drama ended up in the right place – for a long time.

PINK TRIANGLE:

The area around the corners of Duval and Petronia streets was once a hub of social activity for Key West's black and Cuban communities. Today, it's the heart of a gay-oriented district including such bars as the 801, (formerly Big Mama's,) Aqua, and the Bourbon Street Pub. It's affectionately referred to by many locals as the "Pink Triangle."

Photo courtesy of Monroe County Public Library

The Key Wester resort, as it appeared in the early 1960s. The cabana The Beatles stayed in is the third one down from the top.

Here Today ... Gone Tomorrow

And so I quit the police department,
and got myself a steady job.
And though she tried her best to help me,
she could steal but she could not rob.
– 'She Came In Through The Bathroom Window,' by The Beatles

Celebrities are nothing new to the Keys.

Besides obvious names such as Ernest Hemingway and Jimmy Buffett, the likes of Bogart and Bacall, Bill Clinton, Oprah Winfrey, Johnny Carson, Roy Scheider, William Shatner, Wayne Newton, Hulk Hogan and many, many more famous writers, musicians, movie stars, sports legends and politicians have all lived, vacationed, or worked down here at one time or another.

For many locals of a certain age, though, the ultimate Key West celebrity sighting took place in early September of 1964 when The Beatles paid their first and only visit to the Southernmost City.

The inside scoop on the peculiar crime that transpired during their stay here never really made the local papers, but it's forever etched in the mind of legendary former Key West Police Detective Emilio "Duke" Yannacone, who helped show the Fab Four around Key West.

A Key West cop for nearly four decades, Yannacone retired from the force in 1998 to take a steady job as a radio DJ in Port St. Lucie, Florida. But he's never stopped speculating as to who might have broken into The Beatles' suites at the Key Wester Inn on South Roosevelt Boulevard and how they managed to make off with some very valuable souvenirs.

In September of 1964, The Beatles had the world at their feet. Unheard of in America 12 months earlier, the band was now in the midst of its whirlwind first U.S. tour following their well-publicized landing at JFK Airport in New York City and their subsequent appearance on the Ed Sullivan Show. The Fab Four's first feature film "A Hard Days Night" had just opened at the Strand Theatre on Duval Street when it was announced by a Key West radio station that the band, en route to a gig in Jacksonville from one in Montreal, had been diverted by Hurricane Dora, then bearing down on north Florida.

For reasons that are still not entirely clear, The Beatles ended up coming to Key West to while away a couple of days. And as you might imagine, security was tight. Yannacone and the rest of the KWPD were all pressed into service to keep the famous rockers safe – mostly from their frenzied fans.

Around 3:30 a.m. on Sept. 9, the Beatles' chartered plane touched down at the Key West airport and the band members and their entourage – including singer Dusty Springfield and famed keyboardist Billy Preston – hopped out. They climbed into Key West Police Officer Nilo Albury's cruiser and took off for their hotel located less than a mile from the airport.

The next day, Yannacone, Detective Sgt. Harry Sawyer Sr., and Detective Corporal Larry Rodriguez drove them downtown to Leed's clothing store at the corner of Duval and Southard streets. There, John and Paul purchased socks, underwear and a jacket for John, before beating a hasty retreat back to the Key Wester. It was impossible for them to go anywhere without being mobbed. Back at the hotel, hundreds of their fans wandered the grounds, hid in bushes and staked out the band's villa hoping for just a glance of one of the superstar musicians. Hotel employees were said to be selling the ashtrays, silverware and glasses they used. Local schoolgirls collected the pool water in vials and sold it.

At the time of the crime...

In 1964 Henri Mae Williams was charged with second-degree murder, after she admitted hurling a 12-inch butcher knife at her common-law husband, Willie J. Williams. The knife severed an artery in Willie's leg and he bled to death.

And though they were here on vacation, the boys in the band did manage to get in a little practice; One night Ringo and George jammed with legendary local lounge singer Coffee Butler 'til the wee hours at the motel bar. As for John and Paul, they stayed up one night drinking heavily and crying about the fact that both had lost their mothers at an early age. McCartney would later immortalize the incident in his song "Here Today," written after Lennon's death in 1980.

And then, just as quickly as they had arrived, The Beatles were gone, leaving the town in peace and leaving Yannacone to get back to work solving Key West homicides – or so he thought.

"The day after they left, [Beatles producer] George Martin called and said that a plaid jacket belonging to Paul, a light blue long-sleeved, button-down shirt belonging to John Lennon and a 35 millimeter camera had been stolen from their hotel room," Yannacone recalled. "And he said that they didn't want to press charges, but they did want the stuff back. I thought to myself, 'How could anyone get in there to steal that stuff with all those cops around?'"

Eventually, Yannacone decided his best bet was to place a classified ad in the Citizen asking for the return of the stolen items, no questions asked.

He did so and a couple of days later the move began to bear fruit.

First off, the detective received a mysterious package addressed to him at the stationhouse containing a size-7 woman's shoebox wrapped in brown paper. Inside the box was the missing camera minus, of course, the film. Shortly afterwards, Yannacone got a call from a fellow officer saying that he had been tipped off that Paul's jacket could be located at an apartment at Porter Place. And it was.

Two down, one to go.

Not long afterwards, Yannacone heard that somebody was selling pieces of John Lennon's shirt on the grounds of Key West High School. He paid a visit, but came away empty-handed. Eventually, the shirt's collar, emblazoned with its "John Lennon" monogram, was located. That same day, Yannacone said he threw all the recovered items into the mail to New York City where the band was staying.

All the loose ends of The Beatles first and only visit to Key West were wrapped up; maybe a little too cleanly for Yannacone.

"I never heard from them after that," he said. "I was thinking that they would call to say 'thank you,' but they never did. One time a few years ago, Paul was on TV and they were answering phone calls from the public. I tried really hard to get through, but couldn't."

He also never arrested anybody for stealing all the stuff from the band's hotel.

"I have an idea who did it," Yannacone allows.

But he won't name names.

He does say that, most likely, she came in through the bathroom window.

NEWS FLASH: BEATLE EATS CHICKEN!:

During The Beatles' visit to Key West, drummer Ringo Starr enjoyed sampling the local culinary delights. He later claimed that the southern fried chicken cooked for him by local Jernice Reid was the only decent meal he had eaten in America. Reid's daughter Brenda was a member of The Exciters, one of the bands opening for The Beatles on their first U.S. tour.

Photo by roboneal.com

The Ann Street house where Frank Fontis was shot to death on Jan. 5, 1979.

The Mysterious Killing of Frank Fontis

Flamboyant and driven, Frank Fontis hobnobbed with Key West's high and mighty. One day, it all came crashing down …

Largely liberal, tolerant and relatively free of violent crime, Key West is today a haven for many wealthy and successful gay people from around the world. From the grudging acceptance of its first homegrown homosexual population, out of the necessity of social harmony, to its current status as a must-see destination for the gay jet-set, Key West has always been ahead of the curve on this issue.

Celebrated American playwright Tennessee Williams was among the pioneering gay men who sought out the charms of this friendly island in the sun. He bought a home in Key West in 1949 after vacationing here several times and probably enjoying himself at Florida's first gay bar, "The Oldest Bar," where Capt. Tony's Saloon stands today.

By the 1970s, Key West's balmy days and sizzling nightlife created a well-deserved reputation for the town as a gay Mecca. In 1978, the Key West Business Guild was formed. Touted as the country's first "gay chamber of commerce," it was launched to help promote gay-owned businesses such as the many bed and breakfast establishments opened in the beautiful old gingerbread houses these incoming entrepreneurs saved from neglect and disrepair.

But the increase in gay tourism in the late 1970s and the money it brought to Key West was one of the few bright spots in an otherwise bleak picture. With the economy in a slump and drug smuggling on the rise, street crime was spiraling out of control – especially on lower Duval Street. Certain events also suggested something of a backlash against the influx of gays and their increasing importance to Key West's economy. In early 1979, Williams himself was mugged and beaten as he strolled down the Duval Street strip with a friend. "Maybe they weren't punks at all, but New York drama critics," the unflappable playwright commented to People magazine.

Worst of all, in the early morning of Jan. 5, 1979, Williams' flamboyant longtime housekeeper and gardener Frank Fontis, 49, was shot in the head and killed at his Ann Street residence during an apparent botched robbery.

Two drifters, Michael Craig Messina and James Dillman, were soon arrested and charged with Fontis' murder, but the outcome of their trials left many questions unanswered, and left some residents of the island city concerned for the future of their town.

Frank Fontis came to Key West from California in the mid-1960s and quickly established himself as both a larger-than-life island character and a social climber. An organist by trade, Fontis was also a landscape artist whose projects included the garden of Tennessee Williams' Duncan Street house and the refurbishing of Mallory Square in the early 1970s.

But it's his extra-curricular activities and lifestyle that are best remembered by many who knew him.

"He had a big mouth," said one acquaintance who knew Fontis for years. "He wore a lot of gold jewelry and was always making scenes in public … hitting on sailors and things like that. We used to tell him that something bad was going to happen to him if he kept on like that, but that's just the way he was. In the end, it caught up with him."

According to the source, the landscaper – who counted then-President Jimmy Carter's mother Lillian a friend – was a social chameleon who changed colors when it suited him – or his businesses.

At the time of the crime...

Key West police Corporal Pedro Corpion made a name for himself in the late 1970s and early '80s as an intelligent and educated officer – with occasional lapses of common sense. Legend has it that he once ran a red light in his patrol car, stopped to write himself a ticket, and then asked for a court hearing. The judge supposedly told him he should have let himself off with a warning.

"He was in with everybody who was anybody," said the source, who remembers fondly the huge Christmas parties Fontis used to throw. "But these were all people who could do things for him. Frank was a bullshit artist, always hyping himself and showing off his jewelry. In the end that might have been part of the reason he got whacked."

As 1979 dawned, Fontis' life seemed good.

He was a successful businessman, knew "the highest of the high," according to his landlady, and was in the process of realizing his boyhood dream of creating a museum – The Old Coffee Mill and Florida Railroad Museum – on the site of the property near the corner of Ann and Greene Streets.

But there was more to Fontis than met the eye.

In the Jan. 6, 1979 edition of the Miami Herald, reporter Susan Sachs quoted an unnamed source saying that "(Fontis) ... often talked casually of dying, saying only recently that his 'time' might be coming soon."

"Near the end, he was getting into some weird things," confirmed another friend of Fontis, refusing to elaborate further.

But nothing his friends and business associates knew about Fontis could prepare them for the shock that awaited them in the Key West Citizen of Jan. 5: He had been shot three times as he stood naked in the doorway of his home and left for dead in a growing pool of blood on his front porch.

In the early hours of Jan. 5, a young Citizen reporter – who likes to keep her name out of the limelight these days – heard the call about the shooting come in on a police radio as she waited with officers at a Stock Island drug stakeout.

Knowing that Ann Street is a short one, she feared the worst for the friendly man she knew as "Frank" from her walks in the area and she rushed to the crime scene as soon as she was able.

When she arrived at 201 Ann St., Fontis already had been removed by paramedics and taken to Florida Keys Memorial Hospital, where he was prounounced dead on arrival.

© Wright Langley

Frank Fontis at a landscaping job in the Meadows neighborhood of Key West, in 1972.

Officers were busy removing the one true eyewitness to the killing: An Amazon parrot named Coco who became a ward of the court on the night of the murder.

Unfortunately for police, Coco, who moved in with the Citizen reporter after the shooting and still lives with her today, is unable –

or unwilling – to talk. He does, however, become spooked by gunfire-like sounds, such as the slamming of a door, as if recalling the night of mayhem that led to his forced relocation.

As police tried to piece together the events that preceeded the brutal slaying, witnesses told them that at about 1 a.m. they heard a shot followed by a moan and a voice saying the words "Oh no," then several more shots.

One woman also said that she saw two men rush from the porch into a running car then speed away, tires squealing.

Another witness then ran around the corner to Sloppy Joe's Bar to call for an ambulance, but by then it was already too late for Fontis.

Unbeknownst to the investigating officers, there had been another home invasion in Key West that night: Tennessee Williams' small Conch house on Duncan Street, which Fontis had been taking care of while Williams was out of town.

Though no evidence exists to suggest a link between Fontis' murder and the harassment Williams had been dealing with at the time, Fontis' death clearly rattled the famous playwright.

In an interview with freelance journalist Madeleine Blais in the April 1, 1979 issue of the Miami Herald's Tropic magazine, Williams itemized the negative events afflicting his life since January: He had been mugged twice while walking downtown; his dog had disappeared; guests at his home were subjected to the derision of a group of kids throwing beer cans at Williams' front door yelling "come on out, faggot," and lighting loud firecrackers; and finally, his house had been looted twice, once on the evening of Fontis' murder.

"He was a peculiar man," said Williams of Fontis, who had by then been unmasked as the thief pilfering original manuscripts from Williams' house – including "A Streetcar Named Desire." "I guess he supposed the manuscripts would be worth a great deal some day and that he would outlive me. He'd been systematically stealing papers over the course of the nine years he took care of my house."

Asked what he thought of his residence being burglarized the same evening Fontis was killed, Williams replied, "It's peculiar the way they ransacked the two houses on the same night. They were obviously looking for something. Dope, probably. At least that was the first theory. I don't think there have been any alternative theories..."

Following the Fontis shooting detectives had discovered dollar bills scattered around his bloodstained front porch, a $10 and a $20 lying loose on a bed in the house and a wallet containing an another $20 bill. Additionally, Detective Sgt. Robert Lastres reported that Fontis' precious jewelry, sitting on a chest in the bedroom, had not been stolen, though when the two suspects, Dillman and Messina were brought to trial in Key West for the killing, they were also charged with the theft of a gold necklace with the letter "F" inscribed in diamonds on the front as well as $600 in cash.

Shortly after Fontis' murder, the world began closing in on the suspects Dillman and Messina.

On Jan. 25, 1979, Key West police detective Russel Barker traveled to Las Vegas to interview the two men, then in custody for a similar crime committed there.

It was found that the car the pair was driving at the time of their arrest in Nevada matched the description given to Key West police of the getaway car in the Fontis murder. By July 18, warrants had been issued for both men and the extradition process began.

So, was Fontis' murder gay-bashing run amok? Or just a simple robbery that went sour? The answer is, probably neither. "The case became something of a cause celebre because it was a gay murder," former state prosecutor Richard Fowler has said.

Michael Craig Messina was the first suspect to come to trial for the killing. He was acquitted on Oct. 2 of the charges of robbery and second-degree murder by a Monroe County jury.

James Dillman came to trial later – due to additional charges stemming from a prison break while in Key West. He too was cleared of the same charges on Oct. 6, 1980. Another man, Dwayne Charles Kieber, was also busted in connection with the crime, but also beat the murder rap.

The question of who killed Frank Fontis remains a mystery to both the authorities and the residents of the Island City – or most of them, anyway.

"It still is a mystery," a Fontis acquaintance said. "The bunch he was mixed up in wouldn't tell you anyway. He was involved in so many different things ..."

THE PAINTING PLAYWRIGHT:

Tennessee Williams' status as America's greatest playwright didn't stop him from dabbling in other art forms. He took up painting in his later years under the tutelage of his partner Henry Faulker and showed his work at the Gingerbread Square Gallery on Duval Street. Most people agree that Williams wasn't much of an artist, but his paintings today are valuable collectors' items.

Williams' 'David Super Star' is reproduced courtesy of Jeff Birn, of Gingerbread Square Gallery.

Photo by roboneal.com

This historic building at the corner of Front and Duval streets once housed the First National Bank of the Florida Keys.

The Great Key West Bank Robbery

Bank robberies just didn't happen in Key West. At least not until Halloween 1965 …

Despite the brazen and bloody bank job depicted in Ernest Hemingway's classic 1939 novel *To Have and Have Not*, bank robberies have always been relatively rare in Key West.

It's not that criminals here don't have the usual urges. It's just that it's a dumb idea to commit crimes requiring a quick and painless getaway on an island this small – with only one road leading out of town.

Hemingway's revolutionary Cuban bank robbers solved this problem by commandeering a boat so fast they couldn't be caught as they fled back to Cuba. Unfortunately for them, they ran out of gas and none of them lived to spend a dime of the booty.

Right up until the mid-1960s there hadn't been a major bank robbery in Key West.

This would change on Halloween weekend 1965.

Because the federal government insures depositors up to a certain point, bank robberies automatically become the jurisdiction of the FBI. For that reason, details of what really happened that infamous weekend remain scarce.

But one fact is certain: On Nov. 1, 1965, the Key West Citizen reported that thieves had pulled off a professional bank job at the historic First National Bank of the Florida Keys on Front Street. Ironically, this was the same 74-year-old bank robbed three decades earlier in *To Have and Have Not.* Life was imitating art in felonious fashion.

All over Florida the media was buzzing about this extraordinary heist, which would cause bank president J.J. Pinder and his insurance agents a major headache for some time.

The daring break-in was discovered at about 6:30 a.m. on Nov. 1 by the bank's porter, John Stocker. The long-time employee had noticed that a soft-drink machine on the second floor had been vandalized and that the door to the records vault, located directly above the ground floor safety deposit vault, was open. Stocker called Pinder, who immediately phoned the Feds. Pinder then rushed to the bank to see what had happened..

"I could hardly talk," Pinder would later say. "There was water on the floor, old sandwiches and coffee cups, cement dust all over, and in the safe deposit vault, drawers hanging open, smashed and pried open. I kept thinking, I'm having a dream."

Pinder said the robbers must have committed the crime in the hours between 6:30 on Halloween night and 6:30 on the morning of Nov. 1. The thieves had jimmied open a steel door at the rear of the second floor of the building, which led to the employee luncheon patio. From there they broke into the building itself.

Positioned in the records vault, with its noise-proof walls, the thieves used a water hose and cold soda cans from the lunch room machine to cool the drills as they chiseled through two quarter-inch-thick steel plates and reinforced concrete, destroying electrical wiring in the process. Then, they lowered themselves into the safety deposit vault and got to work on the boxes.

There were some 1,000 boxes in the vault, but the robbers knew exactly what they were after and ended up raiding only about 90 of them.

At the time of the crime...

On Nov. 10, 1965, an altercation between two shrimpers left one man in a coma and another in jail. Officers found an unidentified man lying naked on the floor of a trailer "with a side of his head stomped in and nearly crushed." The cops were advised by the owner, Mrs. Avant, to find and arrest her husband, which they did shortly thereafter. The man was discovered hiding on the roof of the Wagon Wheel Saloon on Caroline Street. He was convinced by police dog "Rebel" to come along quietly.

Photo courtesy of Monroe County Public Library

The hole the thieves made in the ceiling of the safety deposit box vault.

"The floor of the vault was littered with rings and bracelets … evidently what they were looking for was cash," Pinder told the Citizen. "They must have had a local guy with them who knew which ones to get into."

The thieves even passed over the solid gold tea service of the Curry family estate – worth a fortune – in their quest for cold, hard cash.

The official statement from the FBI was "no comment," but in the days following the theft small bits of information began to leak to the press.

The prevailing theory, reported in the Nov. 2 Citizen, was that "Heavy equipment, oxygen tanks, acetylene torches and huge concrete boring drills with their accessories were hoisted up the south-wall of the structure in a corner hidden from the street by the drive-in window addition." Three men would have been needed to operate one of the drills, police said.

Construction workers estimated the drilling job must have taken at least 15 hours. Pinder later said he thought the bandits must have spent about 36 hours in the vault itself.

On Nov. 4 with the case still unsolved, a Citizen editorial declared that "the recent bank burglary was performed by Key West criminals," and stated that there was "… a nice reward waiting for the citizen who can help bring these crooks to justice." The editorial went on to denounce certain Key Westers who had been heard to say "anyone who would hide valuables in a safety deposit box deserves to lose them."

In another Hemingway-related coincidence, the FBI had assigned to the case a man by the name of Harry Morgan, the same moniker Hemingway gave to his protagonist boat captain in *To Have and Have Not*; the same captain who was forced to aid the Cuban bank robbers in their getaway.

By Nov. 11, Morgan was still refusing to comment to the Citizen. But that day's edition carried an editorial declaring the robbers as good as caught and calling them "stupid" and "crazy."

A gas station attendant, Virgil Hargis, said he had seen three men the day after the crime in a truck that fit the description of a vehicle reported parked near the bank over the weekend. The men looked Cuban, he said, or Italian. They told him they were from Tampa.

Hargis picked the suspects out of police photographs and said the back of the truck contained wet sponges, conch shells, and an acetylene torch and tank.

"That didn't look like fishing gear to me," Hargis said. "In fact, those men didn't really look like fishermen, either." None of them were locals, as far as he knew.

And there, the matter seemed to end; for a little while, anyway.

Two years after the robbery, the Associated Press reported that two New York men had been arrested in Switzerland with securities that were listed among the items stolen from the Key West bank that fateful weekend. It turned out that cash wasn't all the thieves had been after during the heist. The men were questioned, but later released.

Writing about the incident in the Dec. 1990 issue of Florida Keys Magazine, the late former Citizen reporter Frank "Bud" Jacobson recalled that when the time came for the Chubb Group insurance company to settle with the victims, all were paid off in full. All, that is, except for some of the shadier folks in town.

"One box was owned by a bolita banker, maybe two boxes, supposedly stuffed with $100 bills. How could the bolita guys make a claim when, standing right next to the nice, generous insurance man was a beady-eyed Internal Revenue man? No way."

In the same article, Pinder said he had heard rumors that the Feds had been looking into a cardboard sign with a peephole at the Gulf Oil station across the street from the bank where the Conch Train depot stands today. It seems they figured a lookout had been hiding behind the sign with a walkie-talkie and a clear view of the three-way intersection.

Jacobson said that he had been "smooching with his girlfriend on the bench across the street from the bank at 4 a.m. on the day after Halloween. A former city official later told him he had seen him there. When Jacobson asked the man where he was when he saw him, the man said he had been in the bank at the time. The official's admission convinced Jacobson that he was involved in the robbery, putting a "well-known local character inside as the finger man for the safety deposit boxes."

Commenting on the heist 27 years later, Citizen columnist Herman Moore was bitter toward the authorities.

"It is beyond my comprehension why these criminals were not caught," said Moore, whose box at the bank was among those looted that night. "Even my efforts to get meaningful records from the FBI now have failed. You have to feel that there has been a serious cover-up in this case."

Over the years, Moore, who died in 2005, said he had requested and received records and files relating to the case from the feds, only to find them so vague and blacked-out as to be useless.

At one point some years back, it looked like the case might actually have a resolution: Moore received a phone call informing him that one of the men had been caught with some of the stolen stock certificates in Jacksonville, Florida. He was asked to testify against him, but was told later that the trial had been delayed. That was the last he ever heard of it.

"It is too late to prosecute the criminals," he said. "The whole affair is only history now."

Perhaps.

But many who recall the crime are convinced that someday, the truth about who robbed the bank may yet be revealed, like buried treasure unearthed from the backyard of a weather-beaten Conch shack on a quiet, lonely lane.

Bank on it, they say.

BREAKING THE BANK:

The damaged ceiling where the thieves broke into the safe deposit vault of First National Bank is still faintly visible, but bank employees don't expect to see it robbed again any time soon. New technology and security measures put into place over the past 40 years make a repeat of the 1965 heist virtually impossible.

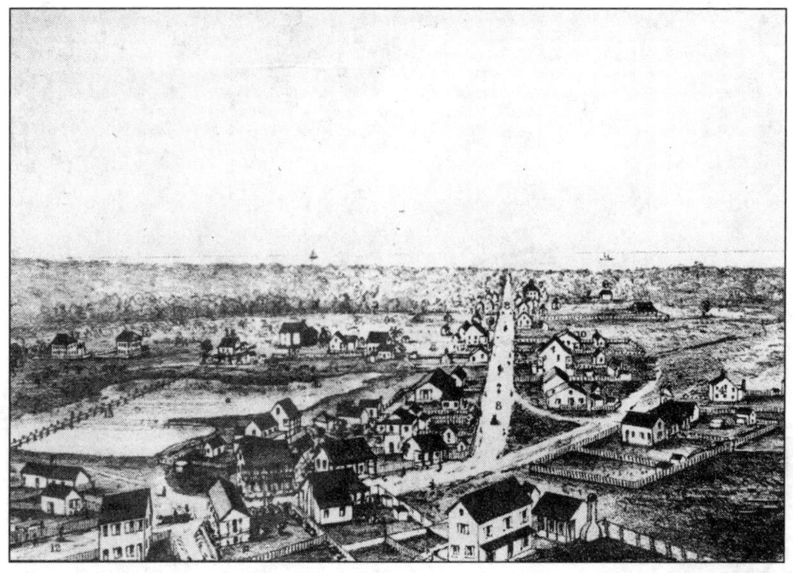

Photo by roboneal.com

This early sketch of Key West shows the pond in the center of town. The Caroline Street footbridge was located near the top right corner of the pond and Whitehead Street at right.

Undying Grudge

Somewhere along the line, these two men learned to hate each other. Eventually, there wasn't enough room in Key West for both of them …

Though the concept is largely outdated today, the challenge of a duel of honor was a viable – though illegal – way for gentlemen to settle accounts in the Key West of the distant past. In those days, the island's lawmen were somewhat more sympathetic to the notion of frontier justice than they are today. Duels of honor, by their very nature, were contests of character, and judges and juries alike often felt sympathy for a wronged man. If he won the duel, he wasn't necessarily going to the gallows for his crime.

Let's travel way back in time now, to 1820s Key West as two mortal enemies converge upon the island for one last fateful encounter; a rendezvous bound to leave at least one of them dead – and a mess for the courts to clean up.

Nobody is really sure how the grudge between American adventurers Charles E. Hawkins and William A. McRae got started. Some say the pair came to know each other around 1819 as mercenary members of the rebel forces of the revolutionary Spanish colony of Colombia. The late Key West historian Marie Cappick believed the pair had met in Colombia, became friends, then came to dislike each other, quarreled and ended up dueling with swords to settle their differences. Cappick's account of the skirmish has McRae besting Hawkins, slashing his face and permanently disfiguring him. But historical proof of this occurrence is elusive. As is confirmation of a report in the Aug. 11, 1829 edition of the Charleston Mercury newspaper suggesting that the pair's "first hostile meeting" took place in 1822, somewhere in the West Indies.

Actually, not much is known about McRae at all compared to the storied career of his famous rival, Hawkins.

A native of New York, the young Hawkins had craved maritime adventure before reaching his teens. Among his boyhood idols was U.S. Naval Captain David Porter, who had been a hero of the War of 1812. Hawkins joined the U.S. Navy in 1818 as a midshipman aboard the frigate Guerriere and spent the next few years fulfilling uninspiring duties aboard Navy ships in the Northeast and in the

Mediterranean.

In 1822, Porter was among the U.S. Naval captains assigned to create the highly successful anti-piracy West Indian Squadron in Key West. By 1825, Hawkins found himself aboard the U.S. frigate Constellation, which was assigned to this pirate-busting posse. Around this time, Porter found himself in trouble with military brass for pursuing pirates with such ferocity that he caused an international incident with the Spanish governor of Puerto Rico. He was court-martialed, admonished and angrily resigned his commission in the U.S. Navy. Before long, he was recruited by the government of the newly independent Mexico to be the commander-in-chief of its naval forces and brought along many sailors loyal to him – including the young Charles Hawkins.

By the late 1820s, Hawkins was a captain in Porter's Mexican Navy using Key West as a base from which to disrupt Spanish shipping out of the port of Havana. As commander of the Hermon, Hawkins was living the life of his dreams; an adventurous seafarer who cut a dashing and handsome figure in all of his Caribbean ports of call. At one point, he became involved in a fervid tropical love triangle in Nassau, Bahamas, which resulted in him killing the local rival for his beloved's affections.

For his crime, Hawkins spent several months in a Bahamian dungeon while the Mexican government negotiated his release.

At the time of the crime...

In 1830, Norman Sherwood became the first man to be executed by hanging in Key West. He received the death sentence for shooting and killing a friend who had attempted to disarm him during a dispute.

While Hawkins' absence from duties clearly annoyed Porter, the Mexican commander forgave his adventurous protégé as he had proven himself to be such a fantastic ship's captain. During one short period of time, Hawkins managed to capture 13 Spanish and Cuban ships escorting several of them to Key West for processing.

It was during one of these layovers in the Southernmost City in November of 1828 that Hawkins once again crossed paths with his old rival McRae, a lawyer, who was by now the U.S. attorney for the Southern Judicial District of Florida.

Key Westers, being an amiable lot, insisted that it was time for the two to bury the hatchet, so to speak, and renew their previous friendship. To that end, Hawkins threw a dinner party in McRae's honor, which seemed to go off without a hitch.

"From that day on, the two gentlemen seemed inseparable," the Charleston Mercury reported on Aug. 11, 1829. "Mr. McRae was a constant visitor in the house of Capt. Hawkins and always received the most hospitable and friendly attentions."

McRae, it was said, even volunteered his services as a lawyer on Hawkins' behalf.

But this state of grace didn't last. By mid-December, gossips were circulating rumors regarding McRae's "indelicate conduct" towards Hawkins' wife.

The truce between the two men, it seemed, was off.

Not long after the revelation regarding McRae's roguish behavior, Hawkins challenged him to a pistol duel of honor at his earliest convenience. The two agreed to meet immediately in Tallahassee to do the deed and Hawkins quickly sailed there to await his opponent. Five weeks passed and McRae still hadn't shown up, so Hawkins returned to Key West on Feb. 7. There, he found McRae and the two arranged to meet on South Beach on Monday, Feb. 9.

On the morning of the duel, Hawkins was seconded by Capt. C.C. Hopner of the Mexican Navy; McRae, by a local doctor R.A. Lacy.

Each man was allotted four shots in the match-up.

During the shooting, McRae managed only to graze Hawkins' wrist with a glancing blow. Hawkins hit McRae twice, with one of his shots lodging in his rival's thigh. The contest was over, but the score was far from settled.

Shortly after the duel, Hawkins sailed off to Mexico on business, leaving his family behind in Key West. When he returned on April 20, he found his house deserted and his wife's reputation in ruins. In his absence, McRae had apparently succeeded in seducing Mrs. Hawkins, and had been treating the townsfolk to the intimate details of his trysts with her.

On Sunday, May 24, McRae, by now recovered from his injury, was walking north along Whitehead Street near the entrance to the Caroline Street footbridge, which in those days crossed over a small pond. A gunshot rang out, and McRae fell to the ground mortally wounded. He had been shot in the back by Hawkins who was holed up in a house across the street with a double-barreled shotgun. Less than two hours later, McRae was dead and Hawkins was placed under arrest.

Shortly after his capture, Hawkins was sent to St. Augustine to stand trial, probably due to the difficulty Key West authorities faced assembling an impartial jury in town.

But the situation facing the St. Augustine prosecutors was no less difficult: The State had no Key West witnesses and, therefore, no case.

Hawkins, who had divorced his errant wife before leaving Key West, is said to have remarried while awaiting trial in St. Augustine. But that trial never took place. Instead, he was remanded back to the Southernmost City where the territorial court discharged his case – in exasperation, most likely.

The entire episode, however, seems little more than a footnote in Hawkins' career as a seaman and adventurer. At least two published accounts of his life and times do not even make mention of these events.

Perhaps that's because, in 1829, Hawkins' career was still far from over.

Though he resigned his commission in the Mexican Navy shortly after his acquittal and became a steamboat captain for an American passenger line, Hawkins never lost his lust for adventure.

In 1835 while living in New Orleans, Hawkins became embroiled in a plot to help liberate the rebellious state of Texas from Mexico. He helped organize a naval invasion of Mexico, which ultimately failed, forcing his retreat to Texas. There, he was named commodore of the Texas Navy. His participation in a blockade of Mexican supply shipping in the Gulf of Mexico ended up being instrumental in the eventual victory of Texan independence on the battlefield at San Jacinto.

Hawkins had lived by the sword for much of his life, but he did not die by it.

Still considered a hero of the founding of the Republic of Texas, Hawkins contracted smallpox and died at a boarding house on Canal Street in New Orleans on Feb. 12, 1837.

His legacy, as one of the few to get away with committing hot-blooded murder on a Key West street corner, lives on.

DUELING TO THE DEATH:

A victorious dueler who succeeded in killing his opponent in old Key West might have been forced to flee town to avoid prosecution for murder. Such was the case in April of 1833 when Key West physician and newspaper publisher Ben Strobel shot and killed a lawyer by the name of David Pinkham and departed Key West a short time later – one step ahead of the law. He settled in Charleston, where he became a prominent and respected citizen.

Photo by roboneal.com

Murder, He Wrote ...

When the Canadian beauty queen went missing in the Middle Keys, her concerned husband ran to get help. Then he wrote a book about her disappearance ...

Everybody, it sometimes seems, wants to write their own crime book. Yet very few people actually follow through on the idea. And an impossibly small percentage write a book detailing the mysterious disappearance of their new bride – whom they've been accused of murdering.

Such was the case, however, with young Georges LeMay and his beautiful bride, Hughette.

Attractive and affluent, Georges and Hughette had tied the knot in May, 1951 in their hometown of Montreal, Canada. Shortly afterwards, the two French Canadians, both in their early twenties, spent their honeymoon in Miami Beach. So well off and lucky in love were they, that just one year later they were ready for a second honeymoon in the sunny climes of South Florida.

This time around, Georges decided to take his wife fishing in the Florida Keys. The events that followed produced one of the strangest cases on record in Monroe County.

On the afternoon of Jan. 5, 1952, the headline of the Key West Citizen screamed "Miss Canada Feared Abducted on Keys: Hubby Questioned."

According to the story, the couple had been fishing off a bridge 12 miles north of Marathon the previous night when Hughette LeMay had disappeared. An anxious Georges LeMay, who claimed not to be able to speak much English, told the paper through an interpreter that his wife had left him to walk to their car parked about 150 meters away, and never returned.

He hadn't seen any trace of her since.

While the authorities could appreciate Georges LeMay's concern for his missing wife's welfare, they were troubled by several facts in the case. First off, since Hughette had gone missing a mere 15 minute drive from Marathon, why had Georges opted instead to travel to Tavernier, some 40 miles north, to report her missing? Secondly, why, after reporting her missing, had Georges told them that he was going to Miami "to get help?"

Tavernier Sheriff's Deputy James O. Barker had agreed to let LeMay travel to the mainland, but told him to be back in Tavernier at 6 a.m. the next day so he could drive him to Key West for questioning.

The next morning, Georges LeMay was a no-show. Early that day, Miami police had been called to an odd disturbance at a gas station where they found Georges LeMay in a state of confusion. LeMay mentioned his wife's disappearance and then "went berserk and attacked one of the patrolmen," according to the arrest report. He was taken to Jackson Memorial Hospital and then transported to the Miami Retreat, a facility for the mentally disturbed. He was picked there up by Deputy Barker for the trip down the Keys. The Citizen reported that Georges had also "become violent" when newspaper photographers had attempted to take his picture in Miami.

Later that day, LeMay was questioned for two and a half hours by Justice of the Peace Roy Hamlin and State Attorney J. Lancelot Lester. But with no body and no motive the investigators were still focused on finding Hughette alive. Both Lester and Hamlin seemed convinced of LeMay's innocence.

Meanwhile, a massive manhunt was underway in the Middle Keys. Spotter planes flew all over the area and search party was formed. But they could find no sign of the missing girl.

The day after George LeMay was questioned, Hughette's brother Raymond Daoust arrived in Miami and offered the public a $500 reward for clues to the mystery. This was a nice chunk of change back then and reports of sightings from as far off as Alabama and Mississippi began rolling in.

The Key West Police Academy opened in 1952.

LeMay continued to tell the same story: Hughette and he had been fishing from Tom's Viaduct No. 4 when she decided to walk to their car and change out of the shorts and bra she was wearing. When she didn't return, Georges said, he went to the car and found the clothes she was wearing and noticed that the clothes she had intended to wear were missing.

Georges said his wife often teased him and he thought she might have been hiding to play a joke on him. He called out to her for a while and then became worried. Shortly afterward, he filed his report in Tavernier then drove to Miami.

Meanwhile, back in Canada, the prominent and well-connected family of Hughette Daoust LeMay began to pull some strings. Police chiefs from Montreal and the provincial capital of Quebec City lobbied the Florida cops to do all they could – to no avail. On Jan. 10, the Citizen reported that Sheriff Berlin Sawyer had told them there was nothing to report. Sawyer refused comment, citing "political repercussions." For the first time, the paper confirmed, "authorities seem to believe the Canadian beauty probably is dead."

By Jan. 18 Miami police detectives had joined the search, assisted by Raymond Daoust and Roger Nedeau, a Montreal private eye hired by the Daoust family. But on Jan. 24, LeMay, Nedeau and Daoust all returned to Montreal empty handed with LeMay, all the while expressing hope that he would hear from his wife "sooner or later."

At this point, the authorities began searching along the "Tamiami Trail," which links Miami with Fort Myers through the Everglades.

Flash forward three months to March 20.

That morning, Deputy Sheriff Barker testified before a grand jury in Key West that he believed "Mrs. LeMay is dead and … she was the victim of an act of violence." Also present at the hearing were Dr. Dophe Perron, Hughette's godfather and uncle, and his friend Dr. Alfred Quenneville, the famed former chief of detectives of the Quebec Provincial Police in Montreal. Both were there to testify voluntarily before the court. They were asked about and refused to comment on reports that "...a shovel is missing and that a blood-stained robe was found buried along a Tamiami Trail bridge." This evidence was to be brought before the jury.

Adding further to the intrigue was a phone call Citizen reporters received on March 22 from one of their counterparts at the Le Petit Journal de Montreal newspaper. LeMay had been "quite a playboy" before his marriage, according to the Journal reporter, and was currently goofing off in the Laurentian Mountains, a resort area near Montreal. LeMay wasn't even planning a trip back to see the grand jury in Key West and hadn't received a subpoena yet anyway.

By March 28, the legal process was grinding along without his help. The grand jury agreed with Detective Barker that Hughette had met with foul play and that Georges could "materially aid in the solution of her disappearance," if he would to return to the Southernmost City.

Perhaps weighing the possibility of the death penalty should he be found guilty of his wife's murder, LeMay opted instead to remain in the Laurentians. On March 28 he refused a direct invitation to appear before the Key West body, citing personal issues with Deputy Barker. The officer had been antagonistic towards him during their first meeting and had attempted to force him to take a lie detector test on the spot, LeMay said.

The case drifted for 10 months, but picked up in October. LeMay's nemesis Barker resigned as deputy sheriff on Oct. 24, claiming ill health.

The next day, LeMay told a Citizen reporter that he had written a 100-page book about the whole affair. He said that it proved Hughette was still alive and that he was guilty of nothing more than loving an errant wife. He planned to divorce her when she finally turned up. Georges LeMay added that he would be happy to return to Key West for questioning now that Barker was gone and scoffed at rumors that Hughette's bathrobe – which he and other members of the Tamiami Trail posse were alleged to have found – was blood-stained. The blood was all in the minds of the police, he said.

Then, LeMay caught an unexpected, and possibly undeserved, break.

On Dec. 26, Barker's son, Duane, 24, himself a law enforcement officer, shot and killed his father during a desperate struggle for a gun. Young Barker said the skirmish had been brought on by his father's addiction to illegal drugs.

"It is the climax to a long bout my father had with narcotics," said Duane. "He would take any kind of dope he could get his hands on, morphine, codeine, paradoric…"

This development tarnished the late deputy's stature and further clouded the LeMay case, which was growing cooler all the time.

The day after the Barker shooting, LeMay finally agreed to return to Key West to be interviewed, but was thwarted, strangely enough, by the authorities: The border guards at the Champlain, N.Y. border crossing refused his entry by car, on New Year's Eve, 1952. "One reason for his barring may have been that LeMay declared his intention of going to Cuba," for a vacation, the Canadian authorities said. "It is more complicated for a Canadian to enter the Island Republic than [for a citizen of] the U.S."

Indignant now, LeMay refused to attempt the trip again, saying, "Now I won't go by myself and if I do go, all expenses will have to be paid." This struck a chord with the cash-strapped State Attorney's Office, who offered a terse "no comment," when asked if they'd foot the bill for George's journey.

Rumors swirled, but the story dropped out of sight.

That is, until Aug. 28, 1957 when LeMay was arrested in Montreal. This time, his legal woes included charges of "Interfering with a police officer … and intimidating a woman." There was also "an investigation of his possible connection with the disappearance of a husky Montreal man … who was awaiting trial on a narcotics charge."

In 1959, on the seventh anniversary of Hughette LeMay's disappearance, the Citizen took one last stab at the story: "Some of thep-peculiar facts are recalled … [Georges] LeMay … drove to Tavernier to report his wife's disappearance … he was never able to satisfactorily account for the full time which elapsed between his departure from the Upper Keys and his arrival at the service station." LeMay had led investigators to a "blood stained sheet bearing the LeMay laundry marks (monograms)." He was also unable to account for his snow shovel, which was mandatory gear for all Canadian motorists at the time. And lastly, it was puzzling that LeMay, who claimed to speak only French, was able to swear like an English trooper at a photographer outside the Miami State Attorney's Office on that January day, back in 1952.

Since that last Citizen story there has been silence. Investigators long ago gave up trying to figure out what really happened to Hughette LeMay.

Perhaps the answer lies somewhere within the 100 time-worn pages of LeMay's book as it sits collecting dust on a darkened corner shelf of some Montreal library.

The book's title?

"Je Suis Coupable," French for "I Am Guilty."

BOOKED:

Early on in the LeMay investigation, veteran Montreal police reporter Al Palmer, who had worked for the Key West Citizen from August 1951 through January of '52, became a staunch supporter of Georges LeMay. At one point, Palmer called The Citizen and offered his services as a correspondent. "Tell [Citizen Publisher] Norman [Artman] I'll make a fast translation of LeMay's book and shoot down a review for the Citizen," he told the paper on Nov. 10.

Photo courtesy of Monroe County Public Library

A hooded Fred Ewert prepares to be executed on Dec. 2, 1904 in a yard outside the Monroe County Courthouse and jail.

The Last Execution

Fred Ewert killed a man with an axe for calling him a 'beat.' On Dec. 2, 1904, he became the last person to be executed in Monroe County…

Young Key West fisherman Fred Ewert had a short fuse – and a flair for poetry.

The last criminal executed in Monroe County, Ewert, 22, stood trial for a particularly grisly murder in Key West during the fall of 1904. And though the poem he wrote shortly before his death betrays a bittersweet view of his punishment, Ewert told his fellow prisoners, the judge and the sheriff that he accepted his fate and was ready to die, which he did at 11:22 a.m. on Dec. 2, 1904.

Few details are available on the specifics of Fred Ewert's life except that he was often broke. On the evening of May 18, 1904, Ewert encountered a man by the name of Frank Whitaker who showed him a rather large wad of bills he had come into by unspecified means.

The hungry Ewert inquired whether Whitaker could spring for some chowder on a boat in the harbor, a request to which Whitaker complied. As the two men waited on board for their food to be cooked, Ewert asked Whitaker for money to buy some bread.

According to the Florida Times-Union of December 6, 1904, "Whitaker cursed him, and said he was a "beat." This enraged Ewert, who attacked Whitaker with an axe, killing him and throwing his body into the harbor. Next morning the body was found and several arrests were made."

After returning from his dinner on the schooner, Ewert began living it up with the cash he had just stolen from Whitaker.

He rented a hack and rode around Key West spending his money like a drunken sailor, at one point stopping at a coffee shop to give the owner a few hundred dollars to hang on to for him.

This was a lot of money in 1904 and as word got around town what had happened, Ewert's actions that night began to make sense to the authorities.

He was arrested the next day and soon confessed to his crime.

Given an early trial, Ewert was convicted of murder and sentenced to death, a decision the state Supreme Court upheld later that year. Apparently, the authorities didn't spend a lot of time on appeals back then.

Fred Ewert made no appeals for leniency and his execution was set for 11 a.m. Dec. 2.

As he awaited execution in the Monroe County Jail on Whitehead Street, Ewert composed a poem describing his crime and his opinion of the punishment. Though he expressed some disdain for the other two inhabitants of Death Row, Simon Reyes and Herbie "Dutchy" Melbourne, he also expressed remorse for his crime and attempted to warn others who would follow in his footsteps.

As the day of his hanging approached, Ewert seemed at peace with himself and his fate. He spent the morning of Dec. 2 quietly, allowing just one visitor, a Father Suebelin, to come and pray with him.

The door to his cell was unlocked at precisely 11 a.m. and the condemned man left it for the last time. He received permission to bid farewell to the other doomed prisoners, chatting with them for several moments before being led out to the gallows.

The last execution in Monroe County attracted a large crowd.

Just outside the fenced-in yard, the curious gathered to gape as Ewert spoke briefly with the doctors who would soon pronounce him dead.

The condemned man then said a few additional prayers with Father Suebelin. When the prayers were concluded he turned to face Sheriff Richard T. Hicks and informed him that he was ready.

At the time of the crime...

At the turn of the 19th century, the Key West police force consisted of 13 male officers.

According to an account written by former Key West Citizen reporter Earl Adams in the 1960s, Ewert "gazed out on the throng of spectators who were clamoring for a front-row view and said in a clear, firm voice: "I am about to die for all future murders in Monroe County."

Deputy Sheriff Sands then prepared Ewert for his execution, tying his hands and feet and placing a black hood over his head. According to Adams' account, Ewert had a smile on his lips as the hood was pulled down over his face. He took his place on the platform.

Again, from the Florida Times-Union of Dec. 6, 1904: "Freddie Ewert aged twenty-two, paid the penalty of the law at 11:22 Friday morning in the enclosure of the county jail. In the fall his neck was broken and he did not move a muscle ... At 11:22 Sheriff Hicks pulled the catch and the unfortunate man was launched into eternity. Ten minutes and twenty-two seconds after he fell, Drs. Fogarty, Light and Gardner pronounced him dead, and the body was cut down and turned over to undertaker Lopez for burial."

Fred Ewert's execution was a notable occurrence in the annals of Monroe County criminal justice in two regards: Not only was he the last prisoner executed in the county, but he was also the last criminal put to death for crimes committed in Monroe County for nearly a century.

Since 1904, all executions take place at the state prison in Starke, just south of Jacksonville. The first and only execution to date for a Keys-related crime at Starke took place in June of 1991.

The following is a poem written by the condemned man, Fred Ewert. It appeared in the Key West Inter-Ocean newspaper sometime during the fall of 1904.

It was on the 18th night of May,
When I threw my life away,
I thought it would not be known,
Now here I am alone,
To suffer what it may be,
But God bless the penalty,
I am not punished too severe,

For the law has done its best,
When I sit and think,
With my good instinct;
And when the clock does roar
In my life there seems a flaw.
I have come to the point
Where I must think deep,

And prepare a place to sleep,
For time is drawing near,
And I surely must prepare.
I know my soul is in a bad state,
And I must make no mistake,
If I have to leave this dreadful earth,
I will not go in a flirt.
Some people seem to sympathize,
But they really can't comprize,
What makes me feel so sad,
And makes me feel so bad,
Is to see that there were three
That were charged like me,
And were let off without a fine.
It might be right,
But it ain't so in my sight,
Now look at this with a sigh,
And see if I was justified.
Don't take this as an insult,
It is a parting ones consult,
Now take this as a warning,
All that think you are on top,
And take care that you are not
Placed in this very spot.
I am sorry for the punishment,
Here on earth.
But when I die,
And have the pleasure to speak,
On what has passed within
This wicked life,
Only trouble and strife,
While there is life there
I hope they say
Now it is for the Governor to say
It is the people who know
And they know it is not right.
For such a young boy
To be cast from this earth.
It looks like a piece of dirt,
To look at what has been done.
But I must keep mum,
And I must pay the cost
Of the other soul that's lost.
The day of my sentence
I took it as a penance.
Judge Wall done his duty,
As the verdict did command,
To be thrown without mercy
At his hand.
But three of the jury
Tried to hang for mercy
But the most of them
Seemed to be thirsty.
But I must look to God for mercy,
As here on earth I have none.
All I can do is keep mum.
The Christians come to my cell
To teach me the pain of hell.
But people of good faith
Take steps in this mistake
And see if this is right,
To try and take my life.
I beg all who have done wrong
Not to look at me with scorn
That would cause the death
of my mother
And God would charge them
with another.
I am glad to see the people
Take interest in my soul
I hope they will never get in the hole.
Lawyer Roberts did his best
As the judge himself said
There was not a single stone
That he did not test.
The sheriff seems to take it sad,
His children may get bad.
For high is the sheriff, high and mighty,
And his duty cannot slight.
So I will say to the young,
For them to keep mum.
Obey your parents what they say,
And you'll never go astray.
When my parents talked to me,
I thought it all in vain,
But now I've come to see,
That I have got the stain.
It seems to be a made-up thing
To put me to the string,
My chances were scant,
There was nothing they would grant.
They even tried me first,
To prevent an outburst.
For it was a made-up thing,
To give Toby 2 years in Sing-Sing.
They knew if he was tried,

And got off with two years,
They would never get a jury,
To hang me by my ears.
It is left to God to say,
If I was justified,
But if it is God's will,
I am sure it is the best.
Take this in consideration,
Remember rum was the instigation,
It shoulds be the people desire,
This little piece to admire.
Everybody's heart has a string,
And this little piece might hit
that string.
So I will come to a close.
To all who knowns in sorrow deep,
And ask the world to keep out,
Of my footsteps deep.

SO' MO' ROW:

The other two prisoners who waited on Key West's Death Row with Fred Ewert were eventually reprieved by the state governor; one of them had his sentence commuted to life. The other, Herbert "Dutchy" Melbourne, received a new trial altogether, resulting in a surprising outcome. His story is recounted in "The Murder of Clarence Till."

Photo courtesy of Monroe County Sheriff's Office

Monroe County Sheriff's Deputy Frankie Hernandez uncovers stolen cash stashed in a water heater at the home of Sam Cagnina on Aug. 7, 1960.

Bad Lieutenant – Worse Criminal

From armed robbery to murder, the 'Fat Man' did it all. Eventually, it all caught up with him …

This is the story of an inept cop who became an equally inept criminal.

Actually, the former officer in question was a corrupt policeman who became an incompetent Mafioso, yet one who somehow managed to tie up the law enforcement agencies and court systems of Monroe County, the Bahamas, and the United States for years. During his lengthy crime spree, this pugnacious, unprincipled man broke just about every law in the books. So outrageous were his antics, in fact, that mention of them still elicits laughter from old-timers such as the retired cops who trade stories most mornings at the Riviera Coffee Shop on Flagler Avenue in Key West.

It all began late in the evening of Aug. 7, 1960, when county sheriff's deputies swooped down upon the George Allen Apartments home of Key West resident Sam Cagnina, for a search of the premises.

The cops were acting on the eyewitness account of the owner of the Ringside Billiards Parlor at 922 Truman Ave. The owner swore Cagnina was the man who earlier in the evening had held up a card game on his premises disguised with only a red scarf covering his face.

After a short search of Cagnina's apartment, the police found, inside a water heater, the $804 reported stolen at the pool hall as well as a pair of cut women's nylons conveniently tied in a knot as if they had been used as a mask.

This last item was of particular interest to the officers as the town's Western Union office, then located at the corner of Telegraph Lane and Greene Street, had been robbed of an empty box that same week by a man wearing a similar nylon over his head.

And so, Cagnina was taken to the county jail for questioning by men he was – ironically – already well acquainted with. You see, short, squat Sam Cagnina was a Key West police officer, albeit one who was currently under suspension from the force for a variety of on-the-job infractions. But Cagnina wasn't the only person involved in the incident who was known to the police: Among the gamblers robbed at the Ringside was Ismael "Terry Lee" Garcia, a former boxer and city commissioner whose name would again be mentioned in proximity to Cagnina's in the near future.

In December of 1960, the hot-tempered and defiant Cagnina appeared before a justice of the peace to answer the charges against him. Overwhelming circumstantial evidence pointed in his direction, but in the end it was deemed insufficient to prosecute Cagnina. The robbery charges were dropped, and he was set free.

Clearly though, Cagnina's days with the force were numbered and he resigned from his job immediately. "Next time you guys come for me, I'll be coming out shooting," Cagnina is said to have snarled at his former colleagues as he turned to leave.

• • •

Sam Cagnina III was born Dec. 13, 1935 in Tampa to a Mafioso father who worked from the 1930s through the '50s as an associate of the Trafficante crime family. The elder Cagnina was a "drop man," moving gambling tickets and bets up the line of the mob operation. It's not clear why, but in 1958, young Sam Cagnina moved to Key West to become a police officer – and pursue a life of crime.

Though he clearly messed up with the pool hall robbery, he was back at it again with a more ambitious scheme on July 3, 1964 when he attempted a brazen, broad-daylight robbery of an armored truck parked at the Kwik Chek food store on Flagler Avenue.

At the time of the crime...

According to Rule 18, Section 25 of Key West Police Chief Winston 'Jimmy' James' Police Manual of 1970, "Men will not play dominoes while wearing uniform in public places."

This time, the bungling lawbreaker was recognized by the truck driver, Arturo Cobo, Sr., and at least 10 other witnesses as he climbed into the passenger seat of the truck and poked a .38 caliber snub-nosed pistol in Cobo's back. One onlooker told police that he had even greeted Cagnina as the latter sped east on Flagler at the wheel of the truck. Cobo had already jumped out of the vehicle after spotting his son Arturo Jr., who, by coincidence, was walking down the street with a friend.

"Hiya Sammy," one witness was heard shouting at Cagnina as he rocketed past in the armored truck. "See ya gotta new job! Howsa pay?"

Not long after he commandeered the vehicle, witnesses said Cagnina stopped it down the street at another food store and was observed casually tossing bags of money from the truck onto the street. At this point, James Weaver, a civilian guard at the Naval Station who had witnessed the holdup, arrived on the scene clutching a billy club and confronted the man he recognized as Cagnina.

Wheeling around to face Weaver, the masked Cagnina pulled his pistol from the waistband of his trousers and brandished it menacingly at him. Just then, Weaver later testified, a metallic blue 1964 Pontiac Tempest pulled into the parking lot driven by a man he didn't recognize.

Cagnina jumped into the car and it roared off down Flagler Avenue, but not before Weaver had taken down the vehicle's license plate number: Monroe County 38-6440.

Acting on this information, the cops ran the plate and were astonished to discover that the car belonged to none other than Ismael "Terry Lee" Garcia, one of the men whom Cagnina had been charged with robbing four years earlier at the Ringside Billiards Parlor. Garcia was picked up for questioning a short time later, but was quickly released after providing police with a credible alibi. Meanwhile, Cagnina himself appeared at the sheriff's office shortly after the crime saying, "I understand you want to talk to me."

At his trial in early '65, Garcia was acquitted of charges that he helped Cagnina escape the crime scene, but Cagnina was found guilty of strong-armed robbery to the tune of $12,000 and sentenced to 10 years in prison. His lawyer, Richard Taylor, appealed the verdict, however, and Cagnina was ordered retried by the Third District Court of Appeals and released on $5,000 bond.

But Cagnina failed to appear at his new trial in June of that year. He had disappeared and no one – including his attorney – could explain to the judge what had happened to him. Several months later, after receiving word that Cagnina was indeed out of Florida at the time he was supposed to have been in court, Monroe County Sheriff Reace Thompson went before U.S. Commissioner William Albury to request the issuance of a fugitive warrant for the wayward Cagnina.

It didn't take long for this move to bear fruit.

Early in January of '66, it was discovered that Cagnina had been living in Freeport, Bahamas using his real name, working in the construction business and participating in local Chamber of Commerce functions. By Jan. 5, Bahamian officials had been alerted to Cagnina's status and they ordered him deported to the U.S., after he apparently refused to return voluntarily.

As soon as he stepped off the plane in Miami, federal agents, armed with the fugitive warrant, arrested Cagnina and brought him back to Key West to stand trial. Remanded to the county jail on Whitehead Street, Cagnina bonded out on Jan. 27 after a New York insurance company with ties to Cagnina's employer in the Bahamas put up $15,000 to secure his freedom.

Yet, immediately after his release, a series of legal technicalities precluded a quick trial and Cagnina returned to Freeport to the life he'd left behind. And when Cagnina's case was finally called in early February of 1968, he was once again not present in the Key West courtroom.

The reason?

He was already behind bars in Freeport awaiting trial for an armored truck robbery in the Bahamas. A week later, however, having been acquitted of these latest charges, Cagnina was freed and returned to Key West – under armed guard – to finally face trial for a crime he had committed almost four years earlier.

This time, bail was set at $50,000.

On May 16, 1968, justice was finally served when Cagnina pleaded guilty of the armored car robbery and was sentenced to one year – less two months – in the county jail. It appeared to many observers at the time that the curtain had finally been drawn on the botched career of a bumbling criminal and that one of the more colorful and convoluted criminal cases in county history had been resolved.

But it was not to be.

By the early 1970s, Cagnina – now known by his mob moniker "The Fat Man" for his 5-foot, 9-inch, 300-pound stature – was involved with a group of Tampa-area Trafficante family associates as well as a crime group known as the "Cracker Mob." The "Cracker" crooks led by Harlan Blackburn were Anglo criminals who ran moonshine, gambling and other rackets in the rural counties outside of Tampa.

In the spring of 1973, Cagnina was charged with twice attempting to murder Clyde Lee, one of Blackburn's top men. The Fat Man had tried to assassinate Lee gangland-style in Orlando in early 1971, and again a few months later at a phone booth near Tampa. Cagnina sprayed the booth with bullets, but Lee survived, only to be indicted by a Florida grand jury for his gambling activities. Cagnina went on trial for attempted murder and threatening a witness to the shooting. True to form, when the dust settled, the Fat Man was acquitted.

In 1975, Cagnina was also suspected of involvement with a gang that stole checks from the City of Los Angeles, but he was never charged with any wrongdoing.

By December of 1977, however, Cagnina was charged with first-degree murder in the April 18, 1974 slaying of Ronald Yaras, son of a reputed Miami underworld figure who owned a string of massage parlors and strip clubs throughout south Florida. The younger Yaras had been found shot to death in his North Miami Beach home and reports that he had been murdered in order to eliminate him from competition in the massage parlor business began to circulate shortly after his death. Cagnina's alleged accomplice in the crime was once again Ismael "Terry Lee" Garcia.

During the bond hearing for Cagnina and Garcia, on Dec. 25, 1977, mob figure "Blackie" Llerandi testified before a Miami circuit court judge that on that evening of April 18, 1974, he received a phone call from Cagnina saying that Yaras had "gone to visit his father." Yaras' father had died four months earlier, said Llerandi, who was then serving a 15-year sentence for drug-related crimes. He therefore took the call to mean that Yaras had been killed, a suspicion that was later confirmed, he said, when Garcia confessed to the crime during a meeting at Cagnina's Miami Beach home.

Needless to say, the judge already was less-than-impressed by Cagnina's ever-growing rap sheet and in light of Llerandi's testimony, refused to grant bail to either Cagnina or Garcia.

But once again, both Cagnina and Garcia lucked out when their trial in early 1978 ended in a hung jury allowing both men to get out of jail on $100,000 bond.

When the case finally came up again in June of 1978, Garcia showed up; Cagnina did not.

He had disappeared again, and this time it would be years before he was finally brought to justice.

Garcia, who faced the music, was exonerated on both of the charges laid against him and returned to Key West to work as a bail bondsman. A year later he was arrested again, this time for his alleged role in a crime syndicate involving 12 other men, including Cagnina, who remained at large. But, in early April of 1979, Garcia was found innocent of the charges at his trial in Miami and was released again – this time for good.

He died a free man in Key West in September, 1984.

After Cagnina failed to appear at his retrial for racketeering and murder in June of 1978, authorities closed in on a home he owned in Pompano Beach, Florida.

A violent eight-hour tear gas siege ensued, which forced the evacuation of a school across the street – and Cagnina's wife and daughter-in-law from the house. When it was all over, FBI agents and Broward County Sheriff's deputies searched the premises, but were puzzled to discover that Cagnina was not in the house. Puzzled, that is, until one officer, who by coincidence formerly owned the home, noticed that the closets had been modified. The FBI agents broke down a wall and there, lo and behold, was the well-armed and still defiant Cagnina,hiding in a gas-proofed compartment.

The Fat Man was tried and convicted in March, 1981 of a variety of federal charges including racketeering, cocaine trafficking, and dealing in counterfeit securities. Eventually, he received a sentence of 30 years in the federal prison in Terre Haute, Indiana. He later appealed the RICO Act charges, but this motion was rejected by the 11th Circuit Court of Appeals in Atlanta in 1983.

Any chances he might have had for early parole were quashed later that year when he was found to be involved in an interstate drug ring that distributed contraband in a number of federal prisons.

Then in 2002, the aging and wheelchair-bound Cagnina was charged with helping to plot the execution of a car dealer who owed money to one of Cagnina's associates. The Fat Man was acquitted and left to serve out the remainder of his sentence in Indiana where he remains today.

It seemed that the career of one of Key West's most colorful criminals has finally ground to a halt.

ALL MOBBED UP:

Key West is located between two former Mob strongholds: Miami and Havana. The Miami Mob centered around Meyer Lansky who was reputed to be the godfather for both cities and also owned the Plantation Yacht Harbor in Islamorada for a time. Famed mobster Al Capone often spent leisure time in Miami Beach. The Tampa Mob, led by the Trafficante family, was also rumored to have numerous contacts in Key West.

Photo courtesy of Monroe County Public Library

The First Baptist Church, located at the corner of Eaton and Bahama streets, as it appeared in the early 1950s.

A Burning Desire

Baffled by a series of suspicious blazes in Old Town, Key West police began to suspect a serial arsonist. A lucky break solved the mystery – and then some …

With its thousands of closely grouped wooden structures, Key West's historic district has always been a potential tinderbox – and arson has always been a threat.

The city's first "Great Fire," which occurred in 1859, was believed to have been deliberately set by the owner of a warehouse at the corner of Front and Duval streets. At the time, the city had no organized fire department and the inferno destroyed a number of commercial and residential buildings in the area bounded by Front, Greene, Simonton and Whitehead streets

The second major blaze, in 1886, was rumored to have been set at the San Carlos building on Duval Street by politically motivated Cuban expatriates opposed to that land's independence from Spain. Fanned by the wind and with Key West's only fire engine in New York for repairs, the blaze raged for 12 hours leveling 50 acres of the business district and causing millions of dollars in damage.

Burned by the experience, Key Westers took steps to minimize the impact of future fires. Builders made greater use of bricks and tin roofs in construction to help prevent the spread of flames. The town also acquired several more fire engines. The inferno of 1886 proved to be the town's last Great Fire.

It's understood, however, that should a committed arsonist decide to start a blaze in one of Old Town's historic wooden structures, there's little firefighters can do but try to contain the fire and hope to limit the destruction to just one building.

The town awoke to this reality early in 1956 when a suspicious blaze consumed one of the oldest and most beautiful churches in the city. Before long, other buildings fell prey to fires that authorities began to suspect were being deliberately set – by a serial arsonist.

The First Baptist Church located at the northeastern corner of Eaton and Bahama streets, where the now-vacant Club Chameleon stands today, was a Key West landmark. The stately colonial structure had been reconstructed on the site in 1889 after the original church building burned in the 1886 fire. President Harry S. Truman had even used it as his house of worship during his 11 working vacations in the Southernmost City.

Shortly before 4 a.m. on April 2, Key West police patrolman John Yates was walking his downtown beat when he smelled smoke. Following the scent to its source, he found the First Baptist Church in flames. Around the same time, Father John Armfield, rector of the neighboring St. Paul's Episcopal Church made the same discovery.

Aided by a stiff southeastern breeze, the flames consuming the church were also causing major damage to nearby buildings such as the Trade Winds Hotel, Caroline Shop and what is now called the Artist House.

By the time the fire department arrived, both the church and its annex were engulfed in the inferno and Fire Chief Charles Cremata's men sounded the "conflagration" alarm prompting a quick response from Navy and Marine Corps firefighters. These Marines and Navy personnel patrolled the neighborhood with hand-held fire extinguishers, dousing the many small blazes started by the flying sparks and protecting evacuated property from a roving band of looting teenagers. Smaller fires were reported extinguished at the Elks Club, (now the Hard Rock Cafe,) the Red Barn Theatre and a burning couch on a front porch of a Telegraph Lane residence.

Nobody was killed or injured in the blaze, but the church was completely destroyed, with damage estimated at a cool quarter of a million dollars. For their part, investigators couldn't figure the cause of the fire. Parish leaders and the congregation began making plans to rebuild and life went on.

But on Sept. 8, disaster struck again.

In 1956, Key West Police Lieutenant Hernandez was fired for drunk driving.

Another early morning fire claimed the old Caroline Lowe home at the northeast corner of Caroline and Duval streets. The large pre-Civil War structure was one of the most historically significant buildings in town and its loss was considered a great tragedy by Key Westers. Though most of the townsfolk had been strongly pro-Confederate, the presence of Union Troops at Fort Zachary Taylor kept the city a Northern stronghold through the conflict. And it was from the verandah of the Lowe house that legendary Key West society maven Caroline Lowe is said to have heckled Union soldiers as they marched past, waving a forbidden Confederate flag at them in defiance. (Soldiers frequently searched the house for the flag, but it remained safely hidden in a Newell post, until it was discovered during an early 20th century renovation project. Or so the story goes.)

Located just down the street from the site of the First Baptist Church, the Lowe home – which at the time housed the Trade Winds Restaurant and Bar – had been damaged in that fire, but survived. This time, the combined efforts of the Key West Fire Department and Navy firefighters could not save it. The entire top floor was gutted and when the smoke cleared the building's owner ordered the rest of the structure razed.

This fire aroused more suspicion among the insurance underwriters and State Fire Marshal's Office. It was revealed that two smaller fires had been discovered in the building in the weeks leading up to the Sept. 8 blaze and authorities began to suspect that the fire had been deliberately set, but once again, no suspects materialized.

Nearly three months later, on the last day of November, yet another suspicious early morning blaze leveled an Old Town business.

The Jockey Club bar, located on the second floor of a building on the southwest corner of Simonton and Greene streets, went up in smoke causing an estimated $8,000 to the business, and an undisclosed amount of damage to the Tropical Sheet Metal Works shop on the first floor.

State Fire Marshal A. M. Willis arrived on the scene the next day to conduct an investigation. He quickly determined that the fire was probably set deliberately with some sort of fuel material on a small stage next to the bar. Fireman Clyde J. Carey told Willis that the bar's front door had been unlocked when he arrived on the scene.

Patrolman Robert Saunders, who discovered and reported the fire, said he had noticed that one of the building's windows had also been ajar.

As with the other two blazes there were no suspects, no arrests and the cases remained open.

Then, investigators appeared to have caught a break.

On the morning of Feb. 13, 1957, Key West police officer Rogelio Gomez found two young African-American boys hiding in the rear of the Aerovias Q office on Duval Street during a small fire there. The youngsters, ages 8 and 9, said that they had been with two older white boys when they started five recent fires that had caused property damage and revealed detailed information regarding a Jan. 9 blaze at 916 White St., that only the arsonists could have known. They also said that just days before the First Baptist Church fire one of the white boys told them he intended to burn the building down and showed him the materials he was going to use.

Buoyed by the tip, the police picked up the two white boys, ages 10 and 14, and questioned them about the fires. Then the whole gang took the cops on a tour of the city, pointing out fires they claimed to have started – including the First Baptist Church.

Police were said to be giving considerable credence to their stories; it looked like the mystery had finally been solved.

"The boys either have very vivid imaginations or they have intimate knowledge of the fires," Assistant Police Chief Bernard Waite told the Key West Citizen on Feb. 14. But concrete proof of the boys' guilt remained elusive and no arrests were made. Police were puzzled. Were these youngsters serial arsonists – or not?

Then, 10 months later, at a little before 4 a.m. on Oct. 29, firefighters were called to yet another major inferno, this one at the Poinciana Laundry and Dry Cleaners, at 218 Simonton St. The business was owned by Frank Bartolone who lived with his three children in a second-floor apartment above the cleaners. The family was lucky to make it down to the street with nothing but the clothes on their backs before the blaze laid waste to the building. An apartment house next door was also totaled and dozens of smaller fires smoldered within a two-block radius, spread by cinders on the 25 mph winds.

Fire Chief Cremata and his men took one look at the sooty scene and called for backup. Ultimately, it took hundreds of men and seven trucks the better part of a day to tame the fiery monster, which ultimately caused over $90,000 in damage to the area.

The arsonist was back.

Moody

A few weeks after the Poinciana fire, Monroe County Sheriff's deputies arrested a 27-year-old Russellville, Kentucky, man named Billie Watkins Moody for stealing about $150. A check of his record indicated that Moody, who worked in Key West as a caterer, had been investigated by Key West police for suspected arson in the Caroline Lowe home fire, but never charged. Questioned by authorities, Moody, a decorated Korean War veteran, denied any involvement in the rash of recent Key West fires.

Eventually, though, remorse got the better of Moody, who was serving a six-month sentence for the theft.

He sent for Lt. Rene Raiole and began to talk.

The burning of the First Baptist Church was an entirely premeditated act, Moody said. He had arrived in Key West and rented a room at the Coral City Apartments. For three weeks he had cased the church, worshipping in the building and even playing the piano there. One night, he said, "The thought just hit me," to carry out the deed.

Entering the building through the front door, Moody said he found his way to the choir room at the left of the pulpit. He located a candle he had previously stashed and crumpled paper around its base. He lit the candle, left the church and went back to his room to sleep.

"The next thing I knew," Moody said, "I heard the fire engines. I got up and looked out the window and saw that the post office building was all red. I knew then that the church was on fire."

Expressing "extreme remorse," Moody said he had not set the fire "for revenge or to punish anyone." He just had, it seemed, a burning desire to see buildings going up in smoke.

And there was more.

Moody proceeded to stun his interrogator by casually admitting to setting the Dec. 13, 1955 fire at the Roberts Hotel in Miami and a 1956 fire at a U.S.O. club in Biloxi, Miss.

The more Moody talked, it seemed, the more cold arson cases were solved – all over the world.

By March 27, he had confessed to starting the Poinciana Dry Cleaners fire, the Jockey Club and dozens of other blazes across the United States, South Korea, and Iceland. One of his fires, at Camp Drum, near Watertown, N.Y., killed an Army private. All told, the damage exceeded $3 million – in 1957 dollars.

He even admitted to burning down his parents' home in Meridian, Miss., when he was just 9 years old, carrying his baby half-sister to safety.

"I still don't know why I set those fires," Moody said.

Unfortunately for those who'd like to know what happened to Moody following his arrest, the paper trail of newspaper accounts ends abruptly following his confession. Even die-hard local fire history enthusiasts such as Assistant Key West Fire Marshal Alex Vega have been unable to determine Moody's fate.

He seems to have vanished, like smoke in the wind.

KEGGER!:

During Key West's Great Fire of 1859, a man named Henry Mulrennon secured a keg of gunpowder from Fort Taylor and used it to blow up his own house to prevent the fire from spreading. He was heralded as a hero for helping to save the town from the blaze.

©Wright Langley

Key West Fire Chief Joseph 'Bum' Farto is arrested on Sept. 10, 1975

Where is 'Bum' Farto?

Busted for various drug-related offenses, these prominent Key Westers found themselves hauled into court. One of them is three decades late for his sentencing ...

The swinging decade of the 1960s ushered in an era of widespread recreational drug use throughout the Western world. Drugs such as marijuana, once a mainstay of old jazz and blues musicians, and "Beat" writers like Jack Kerouac, became commonly used by the young American middle class. In the ghettos heroin use soared. Rock stars snorted cocaine like it was going out of style.

But it wasn't.

What was going out of style was the largely urban-based hippie movement. Their leaders and idols dead, the Vietnam War winding down, and their nemesis, Richard Nixon re-elected to another term as president, many disillusioned members of the "Woodstock Generation" departed from cities such as New York and San Francisco for communes and smaller communities. With its laid-back lifestyle, natural beauty and accepting port-city population, Key West was an inviting destination.

Simultaneously, with the Cuba/U.S.S.R axis fading as a threat, Key West's importance as a major strategic asset lessened. In 1974 the Navy announced that it was closing its submarine base at the western end of the island and reducing its force of sailors, well-paid technicians and other additional employees by nearly 10,000.

It was yet another crushing blow to an island whose boom-bust economy had already ebbed and flowed on the strengths of former industries such as wrecking, cigar-making, sponging – and rumrunning. Once again, many Key Westers faced a bleak future and wondered how they were going to feed their families.

And once again, the ocean provided the answer.

Not long after the dreaded announcement of the Navy's major pullout from Key West, many island fishermen joined the ranks of the already thriving pot smugglers and the growing trickle of drugs being brought into the Keys became a tsunami.

With its famously tolerant population of seagoing fishermen and hundreds of miles of remote, unpatrolled coastline, the Keys became a smugglers' paradise. The close ties between outlaws and their friends and relatives in the police force and local politics sealed the deal.

So wide open and defiant was this blossoming drug culture in the early '70s, that cars around town sported bumper stickers declaring, "When pot is legalized, I will be on welfare." Sales of luxury items such as new Cadillacs soared despite the otherwise sour economic climate.

Somebody was bound to notice.

And, by 1973, somebody had.

Responding to increasing reports of rampant drug dealing and lax law enforcement – some complaints made by Keys' cops – Florida Governor Reubin Askew asked the Broward State Attorney's Office to look into the matter. They did, and before long, the U.S. Drug Enforcement Agency, Dade County Organized Crime Bureau and Florida Department of Criminal Law Enforcement were collaborating in a drug investigation that reached the highest levels of Key West city government.

The sting, six months in the planning, came to be known as "Operation Conch." Its aftermath has become as much a part of Key West lore as the exploits of Jimmy Buffett or Captain Tony.

At the time of the crime...

On Jan. 1, 1975, New Year's Eve celebrations on Duval Street degenerated into a violent rock and bottle-throwing riot that allegedly interrupted an on-duty police beer party at the fire hall. "I had one beer in my hand," said Key West police Chief Winston "Jimmy" James, "But I never had a chance to take the top off the bottle." The cops used night-sticks, tear gas and fire hoses to break up the riot.

At the center of the story then – and now as it is remembered – was former Key West Fire Chief Joseph "Bum" Farto. Born on July 3, 1919 in Key West, Farto grew up across the street from the town's fire station. Fascinated with the firemen and the job they performed, he was a frequent visitor to the station earning the affectionate nickname "Bum." He signed on to the department as a nozzle man at 22 and by 1964 was named chief. But in 1966 the city commission recommended firing Farto for alleged irregularities with department funds. A sympathetic Civil Service Board – headed by Farto's nephew – saw things differently and the flamboyant fire chief got off with a 30-day suspension. By the late '60s, Farto had come to be regarded as one of the town's great eccentrics. He wore rose-tinted glasses and usually dressed in fire-engine red polyester clothing and gold chains as he drove around town in his bright green, city-owned chief's car with its golden eagle hood ornament and "El Jefe" (Spanish for "The Chief") license plate. A regular at Key West Conchs high school baseball games, Farto would often park his car near the left field fence and light candles on its fender. A devout believer in old Conch witchcraft, Farto believed this Santeria ritual would bring luck to his beloved "Fighting Conchs."

By the early '70s, Farto, like many of his fellow Key Westers, had developed a taste for drug money and was known to be nonchalantly dealing marijuana from fire stations all over town. It was this behavior that, in time, made him a sitting duck for the Operation Conch investigators.

But, although the "Conch" sting was an elaborate drug bust, it all began with a brutal murder in a small Old Town Conch cottage.

In the early afternoon of Aug. 17, 1975, Key West police were called to investigate a homicide at 725 Whitmarsh Lane. Upon the officers' arrival, the apartment's occupant, Elmer E. "Peaches" Wesley, directed them to a bathroom. There in the bathtub, the cops found the bound-and-gagged body of Titus Walters, a known felon with a long history of violent crime, rape and drug offenses. He had been shot twice in the head and once in the chest; and it was suspected, injected with heroin and drain cleaner.*

Three days later, the police held their prime suspect in the county jail: He was 30-year-old Marion "Bobby" Francis of Miami. The murder weapon, a .38 caliber snub-nosed revolver, was found under a mattress at Francis' Miami home. Also taken into custody as material witnesses were Wesley (who confessed to the killing, then recanted,) and another Key Wester, Arnold Eugene Moore, who was sometimes called "Katrina," or "Peanuts."

Through the end of August and into September, authorities continued their investigation into the brutal slaying, searching for a motive for the crime.

Then, all hell broke loose: Operation Conch had arrived.

At about 8 o'clock in the morning, on Sept. 10, Farto had just pulled out of the driveway of his United Street residence when one car cut him off in front and another from behind. The bewildered fire chief was whisked away by several impatient men and his car was towed away.

Shortly afterwards on the other side of the island, a similar scene unfolded: Key West City Attorney Manuel "Manny" James – the adopted son of Police Chief Winston "Jimmy" James – was pulled from a car being driven by a woman named Mae Arnold and busted by the obviously out-of-town cops. Arnold herself was taken into custody after police found slips used in "bolita," as the illegal street gambling racket is known, in the car.

"It's all a mistake," Manny James said as he was led handcuffed from the motel room where he had been processed along with more than a dozen other Key Westers caught up in the sting. Both Farto and Manny James were charged with conspiring to deliver and actually delivering, cocaine to undercover agents.

Not far behind Farto and James was well-known bondsman Manuel "Curito" Ortega (said by some to be a close friend, and/or political supporter of Monroe County Sheriff Bobby Brown,) and

* This turned out not to have been true.

convicted gambler/bolita man Artemio "Artie" Crespo. Ironically, Crespo had just been acquitted of a charge of carrying a concealed weapon the day before. Now he and Ortega both faced drug charges as a result of the raid. Neither man could call their lawyer however. Both employed Manny James as their counsel and James, who counted among his clients numerous suspected drug smugglers and dealers, hadn't bonded out yet.

A surreal, circus-like atmosphere hung over the Monroe County courthouse as hundreds of Key Westers stopped to watch the 17 handcuffed arrestees being led into the building, which in those days also housed the county jail.

At one point, investigators noticed James Stanley "Mustache" Roberts standing in the crowd. A warrant for his arrest on three charges of heroin dealing had been issued during the sting and he was arrested and hauled into the courthouse with the others.

The parking lot was starting to get crowded as tow trucks rolled in with cars suspected of being used to transport drugs. Farto's fire chief car was soon joined by Ortega's Ford LTD along with one of the tow trucks, as the cops discovered that it, too, was on their confiscation list.

Altogether, 18 suspects had been arrested on drug-related charges with seven warrants still outstanding. Though none of the suspects had seen it coming, one of them, in particular, had been a cinch to take down: Alleged heroin dealer Marion "Bobby" Francis was already incarcerated in the Key West Jail on charges of murdering Titus Walters, just weeks earlier.

For those keeping score, it soon became clear what had happened.

Three county sheriff's detectives, frustrated by what they saw as a protective cocoon of corruption and patronage surrounding the drug-dealing activities of well-placed Key Westers, had gone outside their department for help. By early 1975, the DEA, FDCLE and Dade's Organized Crime Bureau were deep into their investigation of Key West drug rings. In August the noose began to tighten. Farto was introduced to a "buyer," actually an undercover agent named Larry Dollar, by a local junkie-turned police informant. His name was Titus Walters.

Using a gold and diamond ring as bait, Dollar asked Farto for an ounce of cocaine, which the fire chief said he would obtain from Manny James. The trap was set.

Even after Francis killed Walters, the superstitious Farto did not become suspicious. He told Dollar he was still waiting to hear back from James, to deliver on his end of their bargain. In late August Farto told Dollar he was having temporary difficulties connecting and gave him a bag of marijuana, as a show of "good faith." Then in early September, he finally came through with the coke, swapping it with Dollar for the promised ring. Unbeknownst to Farto, this transaction, which took place at Key West Fire Station #1, at the corner of Kennedy Drive and Flagler Avenue, was photographed by another agent.

Subsequently, on Sept. 9, the Operation Conch cops slipped into town and, posing as a visiting karate team, checked into 15 rooms at the Key Wester Motel on South Roosevelt Boulevard. There they prepared to pick up Farto and his alleged cohorts.

• • •

After being initially processed on that September day, Farto, James and several others were bailed out by bondsman Ortega, himself a suspect. Farto then hired James as his lawyer and the pair, both soon to be suspended from their public service jobs, began to talk strategy.

Prosecutors, for their part, had to come up with a strategy of their own.

Most Operation Conch defendants were arraigned in late September before Monroe County Circuit Court Judge Bill Chappell. But citing his personal friendship with Manny James, Monroe State Attorney Ed Whorton asked to be recused from the "Conch" trials after a statewide grand jury indicted James, Farto and the others.

In his place, Dade County State Attorney Richard Gerstein, aware of the self-protective nature of the community, filed for a change of venue. He hoped the move would improve his chances for convictions with an untainted jury. But presiding Judge Everett R. Richardson, visiting from Jacksonville, would have none of it. The prosecution would have to present their evidence to Key West juries and hope for the best.

And so, Gerstein's office set about tightening up the cases, trying to leave as little room for reasonable doubt as possible. By late December, Gerstein's second-in-command Edward Carhart arrived in Key West to formally announce that they were dropping some of the charges against James, Farto, Crespo and Ortega, the four highest-profile defendants. But, if Farto caught a break with the dropping of the "conspiracy to deliver cocaine charge," he took it on the chin on Jan. 15, 1976 when he was arrested yet again. This time it was for possession of two short-barreled shotguns that were in the back of his impounded city vehicle.

If convicted of that crime, Farto faced an additional five years in jail and a $5,000 fine.

James, meanwhile, was doing a little legal maneuvering on his own behalf. In early January he took a lie detector test in Miami and answered "no" when asked if he had sold or delivered cocaine to police informant Gary Sherertz. James passed the polygraph, and announced to the media that he planned to introduce the test results at his own trial, scheduled to take place in February.

By early February, the "Conch" trials got underway in Judge Chappel's courtroom. The jury took just 15 minutes to find George Kenneth Carey guilty of two charges of selling heroin.

Next, the prosecution convicted Marion "Bobby" Francis on two counts of sale or delivery of heroin. One day later, James Stanley "Mustache" Roberts was found guilty of three charges of sale or delivery of heroin. In mid-March he was sentenced to 25 years in prison.

The prosecution was on a roll, and the stage was set for a showdown with the major figures of the probe.

On the morning of Feb. 9, court was called to order in the case of the State of Florida vs. Joseph "Bum" Farto. But the fire chief was not in attendance. His doctor, Ramon Pino, told visiting Circuit Court Judge Lamar Rose that the beleaguered Farto had been admitted to hospital complaining of stomach problems. Pino's initial diagnosis was bleeding ulcers for which he had prescribed antacids and rest. But the next day, a court-ordered second opinion said that with some medication Farto should be able to stand trial the next day, Feb. 12.

And so, a twitching Farto finally stood in court to answer charges he sold/delivered cocaine twice at Key West Fire Station #1, and sold/delivered marijuana once at the station at Simonton and Angela streets adjacent to Key West City Hall.

The principal witness for the prosecution, Larry Dollar, recounted his firehouse dealings with Farto beginning with their introduction by the deceased informant Titus Walters, right up to his arrest of Farto as he drove to work on the morning of Sept. 9. A surreal courtroom exchange occurred when Dollar mentioned Farto's reference to calling Manny James to obtain the cocaine. James, acting as Farto's lawyer, objected to the testimony on the grounds that stating his name in the context of cocaine dealing prejudiced the jury against the defense. He called for a mistrial, but Judge Rose rejected the motion. Farto did not testify in his own defense and James offered little in the way of cross-examination of prosecution witnesses. Nor did he offer a closing statement.

At the end of the day, the jury deliberated for just 30 minutes before returning its verdict: Guilty on all counts. Judge Rose then granted James' motion asking for 14 days to prepare an appeal. By Feb. 21, he had filed motions for new trials in the cases of both Farto and for Crespo, who had been found guilty of sale or delivery of cocaine at his trial on Feb. 11.

But on Feb. 16, Farto, free on a $25,000 bond while awaiting sentencing, rented a red 1976 Pontiac Le Mans. He told his wife he was driving to Miami to visit some friends. Instead, he drove into oblivion. On March 4, Farto's wife called the Monroe County Sheriff's Office to report her husband missing. A short time later, the rental location listed the car, which was due back the same day it was rented as "stolen." It was found in late March abandoned beside a parking meter in Miami's Little Havana district.

By March 5, the day of sentencing for Farto, the Taylor-Glore Department Store in Key West had sold more than 350 T-shirts to locals and visitors alike, emblazoned with "Where Is Bum Farto?" Another hot-selling shirt asked "Where's Bum?" on the front and replied "The answer is, Bum's Away!" on the back. As predicted by eight of 10 respondents to a Key West Citizen newspaper poll, Farto didn't show up for his sentencing. Judge Rose declared him a fugitive from justice and swore out a bench warrant for his arrest. Many Key Westers believed he had been lured to Miami and killed to prevent him from squealing on suppliers.

Meanwhile, throughout February and March, the "Conch" trials continued, resulting in several convictions, mistrials and "not-guilty" verdicts in the cases of some of the lesser-known defendants. Though all charges against Manuel "Curito" Ortega were eventually dropped, "Artie" Crespo was convicted of a multitude of drug offenses and sent to prison.*

The charge against Manny James was dropped after it was revealed that the state's chief witness, Gary Sherertz had lied to police about receiving cocaine from him and by mid-March James had been reinstated as city attorney. He quit the position not long afterwards and moved to the Bahamas. He was disbarred following a conviction on a drug-related conspiracy charge in northern Florida in

* Crespo successfully appealed several of his convictions on the grounds that informant "Tree" Moore had lied to the police. Crespo was finally paroled in March 1978, after serving 30 months while "Tree" pleaded out to a to 2 year sentence for perjury through his lawyer – Manny James.

the early '80s. He currently lives on Big Pine Key, occasionally working as a paralegal. To this day he claims no knowledge of "Bum" Farto's whereabouts.

As for Marion "Bobby" Francis, whose killing of informant Titus Walters foreshadowed the "Operation Conch" sting, he was found guilty of first-degree murder on June 29, 1977 and sentenced to death. Despite pleas for clemency on the grounds that while incarcerated he had helped stop gang fights and saved the lives of prison guards, he finally kept his date with Old Sparky in June of 1991.

With Francis' death, the curtain came down fairly neatly on a sordid, yet colorful chapter of Key West's history – save for the question of what happened to "Bum" Farto.

In 1984, Esther Farto had her husband declared legally dead in order to settle his estate and file for benefits and the cops closed the books on his case. Rumors still persist that he was "rubbed out," or that he has been spotted in Costa Rica, Spain and even South Florida.

KEEP YOUR EYE ON THE BALL:

Bolita, Spanish for "little ball," was an illegal street lottery originated in the late 1800s in Cuba. Brought to America, it became popular among Hispanics, Italian immigrants and blacks in Florida in the late 19th and early 20th centuries. Bolita was wildly popular in Key West for decades, then slowly declined. But, like cockfighting, the pastime never completely disappeared. Drawings usually involved small bets and the picking of numbered balls out of a bag that contained 100 of them. In the pre-Castro era, Key West bolita "bankers" would use the winning numbers of the Cuban national lottery to determine the local winners. The advent of the Florida state lottery took a big bite out of the bolita business in the Southernmost City.

Officially, though, he hasn't been heard from since that day in '76 when he bid his wife "goodbye" and vanished into history.

Over time, Farto has become the Jimmy Hoffa of Key West. His story always figures prominently in most modern accounts of the island's history and the tale has been celebrated in song in "Bum Farto," written by Key West songwriters Ben Harrison and John Wells for their performance piece "Key West: A Musical Tour About Town."

The story continues to capture the imagination because, as Taylor-Glore co-owner Paul Taylor said, "Everybody can relate to a Bum Farto fire chief who was busted for cocaine and missing. It's kind of like a future Key West folklore."

Where is "Bum" Farto?

For now, at least, crime buffs will have to make do with the answer: "Bum's away!"

About the author

Photo by roboneal.com

Terry Schmida was born and raised in Toronto, Canada. He moved to Key West in 1995 and joined the staff of the Key West Citizen shortly thereafter. In 1997 Terry became the paper's crime reporter. He currently works as the editor of the Citizen's Paradise This Week entertainment supplement and the Sunday Keys Life section.

Terry continues to make his home in Key West.

Corrections/clarifications

This book is a work of non-fiction and every care has been taken in the research process to reflect accurate accounts of these historical events. Should you have compelling evidence to suggest that factual errors have been made in the telling of these stories, your input will be welcomed and used in the editing of future editions of this book. I would especially love to hear from anyone who can help solve the riddle presented at the end of "A Burning Desire."

Also available from Phantom Press
www.phantompress.com